Not Just for Christmas
The Complete Guide to Raising Turkeys

By
Janice Houghton-Wallace

L178,919|636.5

Published 2007 Farming Books and Videos Ltd.

Copyright © Janice Houghton-Wallace

ISBN 978 1 904 871 18 7

A catalogue record for this book is available from
the British Library.

Published by
Farming Books and Videos Ltd.
PO Box 536
Preston
PR2 9ZY
www.farmingbooksandvideos.com

Designed and Set by Farming Books and Videos Ltd.
Front page (main) and back page photographs supplied by Michael Corrigan
Front page (insert) photograph supplied by Chris Watt

Printed and bound in Great Britain by Bath Press

Not Just for Christmas
The Complete Guide to Raising Turkeys

By
Janice Houghton-Wallace

Dedication

This book is dedicated to my son Robert J. Wallace, who has always supported my turkey projects; my brother Stephen R. Houghton, who helped me with the turkeys over many years and the Forsyth Family at Baltier Farm, Whithorn, who very kindly take over turkey duty from time to time. I am indebted to them all.

Acknowledgements

I am most grateful to the following for their advice and contributions:

Michael Corrigan and Chris Watt, whose photographs make the turkeys look the stars they are; Tony Northrup for the Wild turkey photographs; Quinton Spratt for the Ocellated turkey photographs; Jeni Stanton for the Bronze turkey photographs; Paul Grover, The Daily Telegraph; The Arthur Rice Collection of Poultry Photographs; Elizabeth A. Varney; Mary McCarthy; Dr Henri Woelders, Sipke Joost Hiemstra M.Sc. & Kees Zuidberg of the Centre for Genetic Resources, The Netherlands; Stephen Lister B.Sc., Bvet Med, Cert PMP, MRCVS, Claire Knott BVM&S, MRCVS & Philip Hammond BvetMed, MRCVS of Crowshall Veterinary Services; Sorrel Langley-Hobbs MA, BvetMed, DSAS(O), DECVS, MRCVS, Queen's Veterinary School Hospital, University of Cambridge; David Williams MA, VetMB, PhD, CertVOphthal, MIBiol, MRCVS, Queen's Veterinary School Hospital, University of Cambridge; John Daft BVM&S, MRCVS; Dave Cunnah CBiol, MIBiol, B.Sc(Hons.), Janssen Animal Health; Sara Fillary; Derek Kelly MBE, Kelly Turkey Farms; Copas Traditional Turkeys; Liz Wright; Marjorie Bender, American Livestock Breeds Conservancy; Rare Breeds Survival Trust; Dr Cliff Nixey, Poultry Xperience; Jeremy Blackburn, British Poultry Council; Dr. Nick French, British United Turkeys; Peter Hayford; The Moorhouse Family, Cefn Goleu Organic Turkeys; The Soil Association; Department for Environment, Food and Rural Affairs; Jack Killeen; Agri Input Direct of Moorpark of Baldoon; Priory Veterinary Centre, Whithorn; College of Arms; The Royal Collection; The Fitzwilliam Museum, Cambridge; The White House, Washington DC; Humane Slaughter Association; Sabine Eiche, whose wonderful book 'Presenting the Turkey' inspired 'Not Just for Christmas' and the publishers for allowing me to indulge in such an enjoyable project.

Contents

"TURKEY, n. A large bird whose flesh when eaten on certain religious anniversaries has the peculiar property of attesting piety and gratitude. Incidentally, it is pretty good eating."
Ambrose Bierce, The Devil's Dictionary (1911)

"Most turkeys taste better the day after, my mother's tasted better the day before."
Rita Rudner, comedian

(

Introduction

If ever there was a bird that has served man well since its inception, it has to be the turkey. For centuries it has been kept for the quality of its meat and its decorative feathering. The Aztecs recognised its worth and held festivals in order to induce good fertility each spring. Seven hundred years later the turkey still plays a significant role in providing meat but there is also a growing acceptance that the turkey deserves a higher profile as a majestic and colourful bird in its own right and should be valued as such.

An extremely important aspect of turkey keeping is conservation. The wild turkey, having been reintroduced to its original haunts throughout America by way of a highly successful conservation programme, is now prolific but there was a time when extinction beckoned. The standard or heritage varieties of turkey – as they are termed in America - can be traced back to crosses with the wild and as well as active, they are also inquisitive, docile and, as you would expect from a domesticated species, have the ability to become very tame. Once highly sought after as a table bird, the standard turkey fell from popularity once the broad-breasted commercial hybrids were developed, thus producing the plump birds that we see on the supermarket shelves. When the commercial turkey industry started blossoming in the early part of the twentieth century it was the turn of the standard turkey to find itself becoming an increasingly rare species.

Today, however, these birds have become living gene banks with such diverse attributes that turkey producers could well require in the future. The standard turkey, although not as muscular as its broad-breasted commercial counterpart, has shown a higher level of immunity to disease and stress and is far more acclimatised to a free-range system so it would be foolish to allow this genetic material to disappear. Thankfully, a few dedicated enthusiasts have prevented these birds from becoming extinct although there are far fewer bloodlines than in the past.

Now that twenty first century society is showing a greater interest in how food is reared, along with the quality of that food, the standard turkey is once again enjoying a revival. Although commercially produced hybrid turkeys provide good, cheap turkey meat throughout the year there is a call for the slower growing produce from the older varieties of turkey, just as there has been for that from rare breed cattle, sheep and pigs. Couple this with a growth in the number of people buying a house with some land and the increasing interest in keeping a few turkeys soon becomes apparent.

The remarkable and well deserved popularity of turkeys has also led to them being kept for numerous other reasons; for their eggs, as pets, as exhibition birds and also simply for the satisfaction of having them around. The turkey is a bird which is not only one of the great food sources of the world but is also remarkably striking in appearance, gregarious and full of character.

Turkey keeping is actually very straightforward if certain guidelines are followed. If you do venture into keeping turkeys there will be both good days and bad days, excitement and sadness but this is what has to be accepted when looking after any type of livestock. However, if you do your homework beforehand and attend to your birds correctly once you are an owner you will soon discover why the turkey is such a special bird. And if this book helps more people to enjoy the pursuit of keeping turkeys, whichever type and for whatever reason, then hopefully the turkey will continue to survive and be cherished well into the future, just as it was all those years ago by the Aztecs.

Chapter One | 'The Bird Tukki'

The turkey not only looks as though it could have its origins as far back in time as the dinosaur, but is actually believed to have evolved from a pheasant-like ancestor during the Pleistocene Era [1] which ran from 1.8 million years ago up to the end of the Ice Age. Although the turkey could originally have been a resident of either North America or Asia, it is actually Mexico which is credited with the first references to the bird as far back as the fifteenth century.

It was the Aztecs who originally domesticated the turkey, viewing it not only as a highly prized meat bird but also cherishing its feathers as an adornment. Worshipped as Chalchiuhtotolin, the jewelled bird who presided over ritual self-mortification, such was the importance of the turkey to everyday Aztec life that during one of their festivals turkey eggshells were spread on the streets, celebrating "the goodness of the god who had given them that fowl." [2]

Copy of 15th century Aztec drawing.

The bird continued to gain a reputation for 'the fine quality meat' and at the Court of Emperor Montezuma turkey meat was served in great quantities. Montezuma's household accounts reveal that in one year his court consumed eight thousand turkeys. [3] Not only was it the courtiers who ate well but also the carnivores and raptors in Montezuma's menageries which also consumed turkey on a daily basis. [4]

Peter Martyr, a sixteenth-century Italian historian of New World ventures, in the Fifth Decade of his De Orbe Novo, written during the years 1520-23, gave us one of the earliest written reports on the behaviour of the turkey. Here it is described as 'a kind of peacock' because of the similarity of the courtship display:

"Their domestic animals include geese and ducks and they also raise great numbers of a kind of peacock, in the same way that our farmers raise hens. The females lay twenty and sometimes thirty eggs, which means that the flock is continually increasing. It is said that the males are always in the rut, which is why their flesh is rather delicate. They seem to spend the whole day in front of the female, spreading their tail, exactly as our peacocks do. After taking about four steps they stop and shiver like an ill man with a fever, whose teeth are chattering from the cold. Just like a young and elegant swain looking for the way to please his beloved, the males display the differently coloured feathers about their neck, which, depending on their movements, change from blue to green to red." [5]

Turkeys have been mistaken for peacocks.

Peter Martyr had not actually seen a turkey before and recalled what he had been told by a priest. Hence he seemingly confused the turkey's caruncles (bobbled skin on the head and neck) with feathers but another traveller, the Spaniard Francisco Vazquez de Coronado, recognised the difference and was most struck by its 'great hanging chins.' [6] In 1525 Gonzalo Fernando d'Oviedo wrote about the turkey in his summary of the natural history of the West Indies [7] – the original name given to the parts of America discovered by Christopher Columbus, which possibly explains why the turkey was also referred to as the Indian Peacock. In the chapter 'On Peacocks' Oviedo wrote:

"Although their tails are not as large or as beautiful as those of Spanish peacocks, the rest of their plumage is most beautiful. Their necks and heads are covered with some featherless flesh, which changes colour according to their will and in particular when they spread their tails, when they make it turn red. Above its beak it has a kind of dug, which expands and grows to a size larger than the palm of a hand when it spreads its tail. At the centre of the breast if has a tuft of hairs, as thick as a finger, which are just like horsehair, black in colour and longer than the palm of a hand. The flesh of these peacocks is very good and incomparably better and more tender than that of the peacocks of Spain." [8]

During the early 1500s the turkey arrived in Europe, brought by explorers and merchants keen to benefit from this exotic looking bird with such delicious meat. King Ferdinand of Spain is said to have requested that turkeys be sent from the West Indies to Seville specifically for breeding but the resulting birds provided meat for the table of only the wealthiest and most important people in the land.[9] It took another hundred years before the turkey was bred for general consumption in that country.

Spain was the most likely first port of call for ships returning home from the New World and this is possibly how turkeys first arrived in Europe. [10] It was probably as gifts that the bird found its way into various countries and was treasured as much for being a bizarre looking animal as for its meat. In Italy during this discovery period, turkeys were regarded as an example of the marvels of Nature – *"in gallo opus naturae mirabile apparet"* [11]. They were kept in menageries and were often viewed as a status symbol by the privileged although they were allowed to roam free for visitors to see and admire. [12]

From Spain the turkey was brought to England and it was farmers in East Anglia who recognised the value of this 'new' bird. Attracting great interest and with flocks being bred and developed at a rapid pace, the resulting turkeys where given the name of one of the counties in which they were reared. Thus evolved the Norfolk Black.

William Strickland is credited as the most likely person to have been responsible for introducing the turkey into England. [13] A farmer's son, he had gone off to explore the New World with Sebastian Cabot. A tale has it that strange looking birds were found with the Native American Indians and beads were exchanged for some of them. It was young Strickland's task to look after the birds during the voyage back and for this he was allowed to sell the turkeys when they reached port, realising four pence each. Although there is no actual provenance for determining this it is quoted in various sources.

Strickland lived in Boynton Hall in East Yorkshire and in Boynton church the famous carved lectern is in the shape of a turkey, rather than the more usual eagle. Strickland's connection with the turkey is also strengthened by the fact that when he was granted a coat of arms in 1550, a 'turkey-cock in his prime' was chosen as the crest. To make certain that it was as he wanted, a strutting turkey cock was drawn, possibly at one of the meetings which Strickland would have had with a herald. The original manuscript is still in The College of Arms in London. [14]

The manuscript prepared for Strickland's Coat of Arms. Photo © The College of Arms, London.

During the early years in England, just as in other European countries, the turkey was only reared for the table of the rich and privileged members of society. In 1541 Archbishop Cranmer prohibited turkey being served in excess of one dish of turkey cocks on State occasions. The female turkeys were considered too precious to cook but by 1544 the turkey had become the Christmas dish for farmers and one Norfolk farmer who himself must have reared turkeys, Robert Cooke of Mileham, was also granted the crest of a turkey by Thomas Hawley, Clarenceux King of Arms in 1556. [15]

In Five Hundred Points of Good Husbandry, published in 1573, Thomas Tusser writes about turkey being a culinary luxury for the prosperous Englishman at Christmas:

Beefe, mutton and pork, shred pies of the best,
Pig, veal, goose and capon, and turkey well drest;
Cheese, apples and nuts, jolly carols to hear,
As when in the country is counted good cheer. [16]

During the second half of the sixteenth century, turkeys were being served at wedding feasts and celebratory banquets in Germany and were raised for the royal table and nobility in Denmark, Sweden and Norway. [17] By the seventeenth century it had arrived in India and here, as in Italy a century earlier, turkeys were kept for their curiosity value and amazing plumage. [18] Sailor and writer Robert Knox had been held captive from 1659 to 1679 by the King of Kandy in Ceylon (now Sri Lanka) and on escaping published an English history of the island. In it he implied that the turkey three hundred years ago was considered a rare and fascinating bird and was kept as we would keep a pet today:

The King hath Geese, Ducks, Turkeys, Pigeons, which he keeps tame, but none else may. Turkeys he delights not in, because they change the colour of their heads: Neither does he kill any of these to eat, nor any other creature of what sort soever, and he hath many that he keeps tame. [19]

Having become firmly established in England, domestic turkeys were taken back to America with European settlers in the late 1600s. The Norfolk Black is credited with being amongst the birds which were to depart on the long journey and it went on to play a vital role in turkey history and breeding. [20]

The turkey was rapidly earning a reputation as a coveted meat bird and by the second half of the seventeenth century was being eaten by a wider section of society, not just the elite. Francis Willughby in his book on ornithology, published in 1678, said of the bird: *"The turkey being now so well known, and become so common every where in Europe, needs no very minute and operarose description."* [21]

In England, as in other countries, the turkey also had royal support. George II (1683 – 1760) put his seal on the delicacy by keeping three thousand turkeys in Richmond Park for the royal table. [22] However, when George III came to the throne in 1760 he ordered that all the turkeys be cleared from the Park.

The turkey has not been limited to Christmas celebrations; it has for centuries also been recognised as the festive dish for Thanksgiving Day by Americans wherever they may be in the world. Although, according to folklore, the Pilgrim Fathers' celebrated their first harvest festival in the New World by dining on wild turkey, it was not until 1863 that Abraham Lincoln officially proclaimed Thanksgiving Day a national holiday and the domestic turkey became the traditional meal for the occasion.

Ever since then there has been an annual pardoning by the President of the United States of America, of the Thanksgiving turkey. This White House tradition dates back to Abraham Lincoln, whose son Tad kept a turkey as a pet, which was 'pardoned' by the President from going into the pot. Two turkeys are subsequently taken to Washington for the traditional pardoning but only one is in the limelight. By custom, an alternative is always on hand to fill in if needed and their names are often Liberty and Freedom. After declaring that this will not be the last Thanksgiving for the turkey and its stand-in, the birds are then taken to live out their days in comfort and care on Kidwell Farm in Herndon, Virginia. By virtue of an unconditional presidential pardon, they will spend their remaining days safe from harm. [23]

President Bush pardoning Biscuit in 2006.
Photo © The White House.

One of the many reasons that turkeys were readily available for the Thanksgiving holiday is that they were used in the tobacco crops as a form of pest control. In this the birds are extremely efficient and from the middle of the 1700s into the 1800s the birds were used to remove tobacco worms from the plantations. They were also used for pest control in various other crops and following the harvest the birds were then fattened up for the holiday festivities. In America during the early 1900s it is quoted that:

"A farmer had his oat crop saved from grasshoppers by turning a flock of turkeys to prey on them. A brood of turkeys when ranging through a field seeking their feed go about their work in a very systematic manner, often advancing in a line at distances apart just about great enough to enable them to cover all of the ground between one another as they advance. Not many grasshoppers get by this advancing line." [24]

During the 1900s, as chemical deterrents were being developed and used for pest control, the turkeys' duties largely became redundant. However, even today, turkeys are occasionally used as an organic form of pest control amongst horticultural crops.

So far I have described how the turkey has been revered for its meat and decoration over the centuries but it should not be overlooked that not only was it written about but the bird also proved to be a fascinating subject for both artists and sculptors. As it arrived in Europe during the sixteenth century, Renaissance art was enjoying great interest and attention. Artists were seeking the unusual and they found this in the turkey. Indeed so amazed were these artists that, to the surprise even of the turkeys' owners, the bird was soon being portrayed in various art forms. [25] Giovanni da Udine included a turkey when he frescoed the vault of the Villa Madama

Turkey surrounded by four flowering plants.
Mogul School. © The Fitzwilliam Museum.

on the outskirts of Rome during 1522-23. The Fitzwilliam Museum in Cambridge, has a wonderful seventeenth century miniature of a bronze turkey from the Mogul School of Shah Jahan. The colouring is very striking and painted amongst flowers it shows that the birds were marvelled at for their decoration. Even Pablo Picasso provided a representation of a turkey for the Paris 1942 edition of G. L. L. Buffon's Histoire Naturelle. Unusually for this artist the bird is portrayed in a strikingly realistic fashion, with feathers ruffled and hints of movement which make the image all the more exciting.

During the eighteenth century the turkey was reproduced in porcelain and from decorative pieces the natural progression was to model porcelain tureens for table use. One of the most famous porcelain factories in the world - Meissen in Germany - produced both. An example of a truly stunning sculpture of a turkey is less than ten centimetres high and incorporates both gold and diamonds. It is arguably the most expensive Norfolk Black you could ever set eyes on and was carved by Fabergé. Indeed in 1907 our own king, King Edward VII, commissioned a collection of miniature sculptures of the animals at Sandringham, the Royal Estate in Norfolk, and this very special turkey is now a part of The Royal Collection. [26]

For a bird with such a colourful past there is considerable conjecture as to how the turkey actually got its name but in reality no-one is quite sure, although speculation abounds. The Aztecs called the turkey a huexolotl, probably because of the gobbling sound it made. [27] Once the turkey started to spread around Europe and to other parts of the world, each country had its own name and these would often relate to the various sounds the bird made. Sometimes the turkey was referred to as the Indian peacock which fits in well with a general belief that explorers had muddled the New World with India. [28] The French called it the coq d'Inde or rooster of India; the Turks called the turkey hindi and in Malaya it was an ayam belanda or Dutch chicken. [29] By the time the turkey arrived in England there was already a bird here of that name, the African guinea-fowl. When the origins of the two birds were determined, it was the turkey from the New World that kept its name. [30] There was also confusion when the eighteenth century Swedish naturalist Carl Linnaeus gave the bird the Latin name of Meleagris Gallopavo because meleagris is the Latin name for guinea-fowl, whilst gallus is chicken and pavo is peacock. [31]

Another possibility is that traders dealing with the Ottoman Empire, which included Turkey, were called Turkey merchants. These merchants traded turkeys whilst on their travels around Europe and the name stuck. [32] A further suggestion which seems equally plausible is that Luis de Torres, a doctor who accompanied Christopher Columbus, called the bird tukki, which is a Hebrew word meaning 'big bird.' [33]

*Norfolk Black by Fabergé now in The Royal Collection.
© 2005 Her Majesty Queen Elizabeth II.*

References

[1] R.D.Crawford, "Turkey", in Evolution of Domesticated Animals, edited by Ian L.Mason, London, Longman Group Limited, 1984

[2] J.Alden, Old Foods in the New World, Natural History, 5/94, pp 76-79

[3] W.H.Prescott, History of the Conquest of Mexico, vol.1, Paris 1844

[4] A.W.Schorger, The Wild Turkey, Norman, 1966

[5] P.Martyr, pp 72-75 English translation by Sabine Eiche

[6] W.P.Cumming, R.A.Skelton, D.B.Quinn, The Discovery of North America, London, 1971

[7] A.Gerbi, Nature in the New World, Pittsburgh, 1985

[8] G.B.Ramusio, Delle Navigationi et viaggi, vol.III, Venice 1565 English translatioin by Sabine Eiche

[9] A.W. Schorger, The Wild Turkey: Its History and Domestication, Norman, Oklahoma, University of Oklahoma Press, 1966

[10] Sabine Eiche, Presenting The Turkey – The Fabulous Story of a Flamboyant and Flavourful Bird, Florence, 2004 p 16

[11] A.Geraldini, Itinerarium ad regiones sub aequinoctiali plaga constitutas, Rome 1631 (fac.ed. By E.Mensto, Todi 1992)

[12] Sabine Eiche, Presenting The Turkey, 2004

[13] M.L.Stollard, "Christmas in Yorkshire. The Food They Ate", Dalesman, vol.32, no.9, Dec.1970, pp 761-762

[14] College of Arms, London, Ms Miscellaneous Grants 1, f.58

[15] College of Arms, London

[16] I.Beeton, The Book of Household Management, London 1861

[17] A.W.Schorger, The Wild Turkey, Norman, 1966

[18] W.M.Thackston (transl.and ed), The Jahangirnama, New York – Oxford, 1999

[19] R.Knox, An Historical Relation of Ceylon, ed. J.Ryan, Glasgow, 1911

[20] Carolyn J.Christman & Robert.O.Hawes, Birds of a Feather – Saving Rare Turkeys From Extinction, American Livestock Breeds Conservancy, 1999

[21] F.Willughby, The Ornithology of Francis Willughby, London, 1678

[22] Archives, The Royal Parks, London

[23] The White House, Washington, DC, USA

[24] Carolyn J.Christman & Robert O.Hawes, Birds of a Feather – Saving Rare Turkeys From Extinction, American Livestock Breeds Conservancy, 1999

[25] Sabine Eiche, Presenting The Turkey, 2004

[26] The Royal Collection © 2005 Her Majesty Queen Elizabeth II

[27] R.D. Crawford, "Turkey", in Evolution of Domesticated Animals, edited by Ian L. Mason, London, Longman Group Limited, 1984

[28] Sabine Eiche, Presenting The Turkey, 2004

[29] A.G.Gardner, "A Much More Respectable Bird...a Bird of Courage", Journal of the Colonial Williamsburg Foundation, 2006

[30] C.A.Wilson, Food and Drink in Britain, London, 1973

[31] Sabine Eiche, Presenting The Turkey, 2004

[32] Sabine Eiche, Presenting The Turkey, 2004

[33] A.G.Gardner, "A Much More Respectable Bird...a Bird of Courage", Journal of the Colonial Williamsburg Foundation, 2006

Chapter Two | Breeds Apart

Although all turkeys originated from the wild they have over time separated into three categories; wild, domestic and commercially hybridised. You will notice that varieties of turkey are referred to rather than breed. This is because globally, the turkey is considered a breed and there are different variations that breed true.

Wild

There are two types of wild turkey: Meleagris Gallopavo of North America and Meleagris Ocellata of Central America. Meleagris defines the genus and the second part of the name defines the species.

The North American wild turkey (Meleagris gallopavo) is divided into six subspecies. These are separated by their geographic ranges and characteristics. The most numerous subspecies is the Eastern wild turkey (Meleagris gallopavo silvestris), which, as the name suggests, is native to the eastern half of the United States. The Rio Grande wild turkey (Meleagris gallopavo intermedia) is native to the open lands of the central and southern plains and ranges from South Dakota to Texas. It is the second most prolific of the subspecies.

The third most numerous, which came close to extinction in the early twentieth century, is the Merriam's wild turkey (Meleagris gallopavo merriami), native to the ponderosa pine and juniper woodlands and mountains of the south western United States, from Colorado to Mexico. The Florida wild turkey (Meleagris gallopavo osceola) is found on the Florida peninsula and is smaller

American Wild Turkey

Although basically bronze in colour, plumage on Wild turkeys can have green, red, gold, chestnut and even purple reflections in the feathers. The tail feathers contain more rust colour than the domestic bronze turkeys and can be tipped with a deep rust, a light cinnamon-brown, buff or white.

Central American Ocellated Turkey

The unfeathered head is blue and covered with brilliant orange warts and it has two fleshy appendages. The body feathering is very striking with brilliantly coloured blue and green feathers, each with coppery red tips on the back and tail.

Domestic Varieties

Blue

The feathering of the Blue turkey can be either a light or dark shade of sound and even blue with no other colouring. It is usual for the female to be paler in colour.

Bourbon Red

The plumage of a male Bourbon Red is a rich, dark, chestnut mahogany. On the back, each feather from the point of the shoulders to the base of the main tail has a fine, narrow edging of black.

and darker than the Eastern wild turkey. It is the fourth most numerous.

A fifth subspecies, the Gould's turkey (Meleagris gallopavo mexicana), is found in the south western United States and northern Mexico. The sixth subspecies (Meleagris gallopavo gallopavo) was historically found in southern Mexico, ranging from Puerta Vallarta and Acapulco on the Pacific coast to Vera Cruz and Tuxpan in the Gulf of Mexico.

Wild turkeys have a highly glossed sheen on the plumage. Although basically bronze in colour, there can be green, red, gold, chestnut and even purple reflections in the feathers. The tail feathers contain more rust colour than the domestic bronze turkeys and can be tipped with a deep rust, a light cinnamon-brown, buff or white. The shape of the body is lean and upright and the birds are very active. They are able to fly at up to 55 mph for short distances and can run at up to 30mph.

The amazing recovery of the wild turkey is one of the outstanding successes of North American wildlife conservation. Populations had withered from an estimated 7 to 10 million birds across the continent in the 1500s to only 30,000 in the 1930s. Only sixteen states had any turkey hunting in the 1930s yet now there are nearly three million hunters in fifty states and three Canadian provinces. Habitat changes coupled with vigorous trap-and-transplant restoration efforts have boosted the turkey's present day numbers to almost seven million.

'Making Tracks' is the co-operative programme between the National Wild Turkey Federation (NWTF) and the state, federal and provincial wildlife agencies. Its role is to restore wild turkeys to all suitable habitats in North America. The NWTF works with these agencies, co-ordinating the trap and transfer of wild turkeys. This co-operation succeeded in relocating some 2,359 birds during the 2006 season. To enable such relocations to be successful there are ongoing land improvement schemes taking place and landowners are given advice on how to manage their land for wild turkeys. Since 1992, 2.5 million seedlings, equalling 64,800 hectares (160,000 acres), have been planted for wild turkeys and other wildlife.

Restoration of the Eastern subspecies is now essentially completed, although Quebec recently had an introduction programme to supplement birds moving northward from New York and Vermont. Most of the remaining restoration is focused on pockets of vacant Rio Grande and Merriam's habitat in the western states and provinces. Since 2003, the Arizona Game and Fish Department and the NWTF have transferred 320 Gould's wild turkeys from Mexico and Arizona to the Chiricahua, Huachuca and Pinaleno mountains of southern Arizona, an area where the Gould's once thrived but was virtually eradicated, mainly as a result of unregulated hunting.

Ocellated Turkey

The second species of wild turkey is the Central American Ocellated turkey (Meleagris ocellata), previously classified as Agriocharis ocellata. The Ocellated turkey is found in Belize, Honduras and the Yucatan. It is smaller than the North American turkey, the male bird weighing from 6.8 - 8.1 kgs (15 to 18 lbs). The unfeathered head is blue and covered with brilliant orange warts and it has two fleshy appendages as opposed to the single one found on other turkeys. The body feathering is very striking with brilliantly coloured blue and green feathers, each with coppery red tips on the back and tail. The tail feathers also have eye-shaped markings, making it look even more exotic. The primary wing feathers are barred black and white, very similar to the Bronze but the secondaries are a bright coppery red and the legs are also reddish in colour. There is no tassel or beard on the chest. Although the Ocellated turkey does have a gobble, it is at a higher-pitch than its North American counterpart. It also makes a distinctive booming, drumming sound.

The Ocellated turkey population is declining rapidly due to both loss of habitat and pressure from predators and is in urgent need of conservation. Surprisingly, in the wild it is still hunted for sport.

Domestic

Blue

The feathering of the Blue turkey can be either a light or dark shade of sound and even blue with no other colouring. It is usual for the female to be paler in colour than the male.

There is a very pale Blue turkey called Lavender and although it is popular, very few exist. Occasionally the Lavender is affected by a lethal gene which causes sight problems. This is more common in females than in males and can lead to complete blindness. It is important not to breed with any such birds but in my experience, if a normal sighted Lavender is bred with the Blue or Slate, the problem does not manifest itself as much as when breeding Lavender to Lavender.

A mature Blue stag can weigh up to 11.3kgs (25 lbs) and a mature female can weigh up to 8 kgs (18lbs).

Day-old Blue poults are a yellowish-white with an extremely pale tinge of blue.

Black-Winged Bronze or Crimson Dawn

The Black-winged Bronze resembles the standard Bronze in plumage but has solid black flights. This pattern is the result of genes recessive to the bronze and black patterns and are part of a triple-allele series of colour genes. The Black-winged Bronze is very rare. Poults are similar to the Bronze but the background colour is yellowish white instead of light brown. This makes it look like a very pale coloured Bronze poult.

Bronze

The plumage of both sexes is metallic bronze but the breast feathers on the female are edged with white, whereas on the male they are edged in black.

Buff

The plumage should be a deep cinnamon buff throughout with no black or white markings on any feathering of either sex. The primaries and secondaries are a very pale buff, almost white, and the tail should be a deep cinnamon buff edged with a paler band at the tip.

Narragansett

It is very similar to the Bronze turkey in markings but in place of the bronze colouring it is a light steel grey. The neck plumage is steel grey edged in black and the back is a metallic black with each feather ending with a grey band going to white, the pale band getting wider towards the tail.

Bourbon Red

The Bourbon Red turkey is named after Bourbon County in the Bluegrass Region of Kentucky. The variety was developed by J. E. Barbee in the late 1800s from crosses between the Buff, Bronze and White Holland turkeys. After many generations of selective breeding, a rich mahogany red turkey with white wings and mainly white tail feathers was achieved. It was originally called Bourbon Butternut but not until the name was changed to Bourbon Red did it become popular. In America in the 1930s and 1940s it was one of the main 'commercial' varieties but, like several of the other high-breasted standard varieties, it fell out of favour when the broad-breasted turkey was developed.

The plumage of a male Bourbon Red is a rich, dark, chestnut mahogany. On the back, each feather from the point of the shoulders to the base of the main tail has a fine, narrow edging of black. The fronts, bows and coverts of the wings are also a chestnut mahogany with a narrow edging of black but the primaries and secondaries are pure white. The main tail is also pure white with an indistinct bar of soft red crossing each main tail feather close to the tip. The female is similarly marked to the male except there is no black edging on any of the feathers and on the breast each feather has a narrow thread-like edging of white. The beak is dark at the base with a light horn tip. The eyes are dark brown and the legs a reddish horn in the young, turning pink in the adults.

A Bourbon Red mature stag can weigh up to 14.9 kgs (33 lbs) and a mature hen up to 8.1kgs (18lbs). This variety make very tame pets, are good foragers on pasture and provide excellent meat.

As regards day-old Bourbon Red poults, the head is a light reddish brown with a darker brown mark on the back of the head. The neck and back is a light yellowish brown with three dark brown stripes running from the shoulders, with the middle stripe being the broadest of the three. The wings go from dark brown at the front through to cream at the tips. The throat, breast and thighs are a pale yellowish white. As feathering appears the growing poult takes on a pale beige colouring with white markings. These disappear as the adult feathers emerge.

Bronze

The Bronze is possibly the most popular and well-known turkey and is closest in colouration to the wild turkey. The domesticated bronze was developed in Europe and taken to the Americas where it was crossed with the Eastern wild turkey, the distinctly different bloodlines creating a stronger and more vigorous bird.

The plumage of both sexes is metallic bronze but the breast feathers on the female are edged with white, whereas on the male they are edged in black. This is one way in which Bronze turkeys can be sexed, once their adult feathers are grown at around twelve weeks. The primaries are black with a definite white barring. The tail feathers are black and brown and have a wide black band with a white edging. The beak is horn coloured and the eyes have a dark hazel iris and blue-black pupil. The legs are almost black in poults but become a smoky horn in adults. Although the Bronze turkey does breed true it is the variety most likely to produce off-coloured birds with occasional black and white feathering but also, in more extreme cases, poor quality smudgy markings.

The Bronze is a heavy variety and a mature standard stag can weigh up to 18.1 kgs (40 lbs) and a mature hen up to 11.8 kgs (26lbs).

In day-old Bronze poults the head is light brown with dark brown blotches and streaks. The neck and back have a broader dark streak down the centre with narrower streaks on either side. The wings have two dark streaks in the centre and a dark spot near the tip. The underneath of the poult is a yellowish white on the surface and pale grey beneath. The legs and feet are mainly flesh coloured with some smoky pigmentation below.

The Broad-Breasted Bronze

Through selective breeding a Bronze turkey was developed that had a double chest muscle which produced a far greater ratio of meat to bone. Although the Broad-Breasted Bronze was further developed in America it was done so by using turkeys that had been introduced from England. Turkey breeder Jesse Throssel emigrated to British Columbia in the 1920s and, when settled, imported Bronze birds that had been developed for the Sheffield market. These were called Sheffield Bronze. The broad breasted birds have thrived in the commercial world ever since those early days. The Broad-Breasted Bronze did go out of fashion in the second half of the 1900s as commercial outlets opted for white turkeys with no dark quills which consumers appeared to prefer. In recent years the wheel has turned full circle and Bronze turkeys have made a dramatic comeback.

Buff

This turkey is named after the rich cinnamon colour of its body feathers. The breed was recognised by the American Poultry Association in 1874 but numbers declined after it was used in the development of the Bourbon Red which then became more popular. With so few people keeping the breed the Buff turkey was removed from the American Poultry Association's Standard of Perfection in 1915.

However, the breed was extremely popular in Britain at the turn of the last century having its own Buff Turkey Club in the early 1900s. Along with other standard varieties Buff numbers fell into decline in the mid 1900s when commercial turkeys began to corner the market. The Buff is

Nebraskan

The plumage is white with tiny black flecks throughout the body but the primaries and tail are white.
In the Red Nebraskan (below) the plumage has red flecks instead of black.

Pied

The exposed portion of each feather on the breast is pure white ending in a band of black to form a contrast of black and white giving the effect of scales of a fish.

Norfolk Black

In Britain the Norfolk Black should be a dense, matt black throughout, with no other colouration in any of the feathers.

still recognised in the British Poultry Standards.

The plumage should be a deep cinnamon buff throughout with no black or white markings on any feathering of either sex. The primaries and secondaries are a very pale buff, almost white, and the tail should be a deep cinnamon buff edged with a paler band at the tip. The iris is a dark hazel and the pupil a blue-black. The beak is a light horn colour and the legs a flesh pink.

A mature Buff stag can weigh up to 12.7kgs (28lbs) and a mature hen up to 8.1kgs (18lbs).

The Buff is an extremely handsome turkey but there are very few good examples to be seen. Over the years bloodlines have become mixed with the Bourbon Red and Buffs with black markings and some white in the tail do abound so work is still needed to bring this variety up to the standard it deserves. Although an alert and active bird it is easy to manage.

Day-old Buff poults are a pale creamy brown throughout.

Narragansett

The Narragansett turkey was named after the place it was developed, Narragansett Bay in Rhode Island. It is believed that the Narragansett was originally founded through Norfolk Black turkeys from England being taken to America and breeding with the Eastern Wild turkey. It is very similar to the Bronze turkey in markings but in place of the bronze colouring it is a light steel grey. The neck plumage is steel grey edged in black and the back is a metallic black with each feather ending with a grey band going to white, the pale band getting wider towards the tail. Where black is required there should be no greenish or bronzing lustre. The primaries and secondaries are barred black and white and the tail is black, pencilled with tan and ending in a broad band of metallic black and edged with steel grey going to white. The back should not have any bronze casting. The beak is horn coloured and the eyes are brown. Legs and feet are dark, approaching salmon, in young birds and a deep salmon in mature birds.

A mature stag weighs up to 14.9kgs (33lbs) and a mature hen 10.4kgs (23lbs).

In day-old Narragansett poults the head is a yellowish grey, mottled with dark brown with three dark streaks, the middle being the widest and running from the top of the head down the neck. The upper parts of the body are light greyish brown mottled with very dark brown and the three dark streaks continue along the back to the tail. The underparts of the body range from yellowish white to virtual white on the surface. The undercolour of body down throughout is a light grey. The shank, legs and feet are the same as the Bronze. Although the breasts of Narragansett poults are paler than in the Bronze it is very difficult to segregate the two varieties accurately until they are around 6 weeks old.

Nebraskan

The Nebraskan turkey was standardised in the UK in 2007. It originated from a direct mutation from Broad Breasted Bronze turkeys on a farm in Nebraska in 1947. The plumage is white with tiny black flecks throughout the body but the primaries and tail are white. Day-old poults are creamy white with a dark spot on the head. The black flecking begins to appear when the secondary feathering emerges. Blue, grizzled and red varieties are also found in the Nebraskan.

In the UK there is a variation of this breed which has been worked on by D. C. Harvey which has red flecks over the body and dark brown blotches at the base of the back feathers. Day-old poults are a creamy white with a tan blotch on the head.

Norfolk Black

The Black turkey originated in Europe and is believed to have evolved from American turkeys that had been imported in the early 1500s. It is most likely that it first arrived in Spain from where it was eventually taken to England. Farmers in the Eastern counties, most notably Norfolk, were very interested in keeping these domesticated birds for meat and that is how the Norfolk Black turkey came to have its name.

The body of the Norfolk Black is fairly long and deep and it is particularly broad across the shoulders. In Britain the Norfolk Black should be a dense, matt black throughout, with no other colouration in any of the feathers. On the tips of the lower back feathers there is often seen a slight bronze band but this is undesirable and efforts are being made to breed it out. The beak is black and the eyes are a very dark brown verging on black. The legs, feet and toenails should be completely black, however, as the bird ages, the legs and feet lose the black and change to pink. The female often has short black feathers on the head and face, which are not considered a fault. The Norfolk Black mature stag weighs up to 11.35kgs (25lb) and a mature hen 5.9 – 6.80kgs (13 – 15lb). It has a placid character and is renowned for the quality of its meat.

Norfolk Black turkeys made the journey back to the Americas with European colonists and when crossed with the wild turkeys, provided the foundation stock for the Bronze, Narragansett and Slate varieties. The Black turkey in America also originated from the English Norfolk Blacks. Unlike the matt black of the English Standard variety though, the American black turkey has a lustrous, metallic black feathering with a greenish sheen.

There is also a variety called Spanish Black. There is a debate as to whether this turkey is a different strain to the Norfolk Black or not. To have maintained two genetically different black turkeys over several centuries seems improbable but some turkey keepers with Spanish Blacks do keep them as a separate variety in the event of one day being able to determine if this is the case. Certainly Spanish Black turkeys do appear to be more upright and slender than the Norfolk

Slate

The plumage of both sexes is an ashy-blue, which may be dotted or flecked with black. There should be no solid black feathers or feathering that contains brown or buff. The eyes are very dark brown, the beak horn coloured and the legs and toes are a deep pink in young birds but pale with age.

White

The plumage is pure white in both sexes. The eyes are a very dark blue-black. The beak is white and the legs and feet a flesh pink.

The White stag is upright and showy

Black with significantly more metallic sheen to the feathering.

Day-old Norfolk Black poults are renowned for alarming the unfamiliar breeder. Turkey owners who have not bred them before are often concerned because they are not completely black. The majority of the body will be black but the head and face can be a creamy white, along with the breast and the abdomen. There is no distinct pattern to this and poults can have a lesser or greater amount of creamy white down colouration. The pale colour will disappear with age and as the feathers begin to grow these should become totally black. The poult's beak will be a pale pink with varying amounts of black on it, especially at the tip. The shanks, feet and toes will be black with some flesh colouring as well.

Day-old Spanish Black poults are similar to Norfolk Black poults of the same age. When the poults grow their first feathers though, some often have flecks of white on them. As the young turkeys moult through to the adult feather stage the new feathers should eventually be black.

Pied (Crollwitzer)

The Pied black and white turkey of Europe dates back to the 1700s. It is very alert, upright and exceptionally ornamental.

The plumage of both sexes is similar. The neck is white with every feather ending in a black edge. The exposed portion of each feather on the breast is pure white ending in a band of black to form a contrast of black and white giving the effect of scales of a fish. The back is white with metallic black over the saddle, which is fringed in white. The tail and tail coverts are white with a black band and white tip, so when the male displays the black band is consistent throughout the fanned tail. The primaries are white with a black edge. The eyes are a light brown, the beak a light horn and the legs and feet a pink which darkens with age.

Mature stags can weigh up to 10kgs (22lbs) and mature hens 5.4kgs (12 lbs).

Day-old poults are a yellowish white throughout the body. Through the down pure white feathers grow and the familiar black markings begin to appear at around 6-8 weeks.

There are similar variations of the black and white turkey. It is possible to see both the Ronquire from Belgium and the American Royal Palm exhibited in the UK.

Slate

The Slate turkey is named after its colouration and is believed to have evolved from crossing Norfolk Blacks with either the White Holland or Eastern Wild. Breeding true in the nineteenth century in America, during the turn and early part of the twentieth century the Slate and Blue turkeys were very popular in England at the big London shows.

The plumage of both sexes is an ashy-blue, which may be dotted or flecked with black. There should be no solid black feathers or feathering that contains brown or buff. The eyes are very dark brown, the beak horn coloured and the legs and toes are a deep pink in young birds but pale with age.

A mature male weighs up to 13.6kgs (30 lbs) and a mature hen 5.4kgs (12lbs).

The head, neck and back of day-old poults are a yellowish white with a definite tinge of blue. The throat is a pale yellowish white to light yellow, becoming a yellowish white underneath the body.

White

The White turkey has been present throughout the documented history of the turkey ever since the Aztec period. It is believed to be a sport of other breeds, where the white gene has appeared dominant. The British White, Austrian White, White Holland and, to a lesser degree, the Beltsville Small White have all been bred in the UK in the past but today only the commercially hybridised varieties of these turkeys exist. Currently there is a strain of high-breasted white turkey being bred in the UK which are sports from the Narragansett and are simply called the White.

The plumage is pure white in both sexes. The eyes are a very dark blue-black. The beak is white and the legs and feet a flesh pink. A mature stag weighs up to 12.7kgs (28lbs) and a mature hen 9kgs (20lbs). Day-old poults are pure white.

Commercial Hybrids

A great deal of research has gone into the development of hybridised strains of turkey for the commercial market. Although the intensively kept large broad-breasted birds are immensely popular, especially for the catering end of the market, there is now a wide choice of strains suitable for the free-range producer. These also come in a range of weights from just over 2 kgs (4.4lbs) to around 15 kgs (33lbs). The majority will be broad breasted bronze or white birds but there are also new strains of coloured turkeys coming onto the market that are being bred commercially by taking genes from the standard turkeys. These will be exciting additions to the commercial stock available but should not be confused with the original standard varieties.

Chapter Three | Turkeys..Not Just For Anyone

The realisation of how nice it would be to have some turkeys could strike at anytime. You might be at a poultry show looking at exotic turkeys displaying and reflect on how great they would look in your garden; or it could be the run up to Christmas and you're perhaps thinking that with your available facilities you could venture into turkey keeping and enjoy some of the income that this seasonal meat bird has to offer. Either way, or for whatever other reason you might think of for keeping turkeys, there are careful considerations that must be thoroughly thought through first.

One of the most important points is whether you are even allowed to keep poultry on your premises. On many new developments, even if the houses have spacious large gardens, there can be a condition in the contract that does not allow livestock to be kept. A pet turkey would be looked upon as livestock by the local authorities, even though to you it may be another member of the family. This condition is usually inserted to prevent any disturbance or possible disputes between neighbours over noises or smells and to deter rodents. Older properties do not usually have such conditions in the contractual details.

Depending on where you live it could also be a requirement to get planning permission before keeping turkeys. When I moved to a classified remote and depopulated area of Scotland, I was amazed that full planning permission was still needed for the 'temporary' housing and pens on my land because they were for turkeys and there are two cottages within hearing distance of my land. The reason I was given for the need for planning permission was that the birds might

Some councils require you to have planning permission in order to keep turkeys.

be noisy and smelly and local people might find them antisocial! Fortunately, no-one objected and permission was approved by the council.

Rearing turkeys commercially could well mean that you need planning permission for a new building in which to house them, even if it is just for overnight use. You may also need to apply for a change of use of an existing building, so it would be as well to find out if this is so before making further plans.

Turkeys are certainly great characters and your neighbours will probably become as intrigued by them as you but the stags (males) do gobble and the hens (females) also have quite an extended vocabulary. Once you have kept turkeys for a while you will know what they are doing by the sound they are making even though they may not be in sight. Adult stag turkeys will gobble when echoing other sounds that attract their attention which, if you are in an area with a lot of activity going on, could mean that they gobble very frequently. They also 'chirrup', which is a much quieter sound and this is made if they want to talk to you.

The gobble from an adult stag can be heard up to one mile away.

Hen turkeys, on the other hand, can express themselves through many different calls. They whistle, trill, quack, call, click, peep and purr. Interpretations of some of the sounds are as follows: "It's a predator, run and hide NOW! comes across as a high pitched 'weeing' trill. "What did you just say to me?" sounds like a two-tone click of sheer indignation and "Don't get too close, this is my space!" is voiced as an indignant purr. "Don't get lost. You seem to be going rather far" is a rapid click and "I am lost – someone come and help me!" is a loud low, high, low, low, low, low peep made repeatedly by the one that didn't listen. "That was a stupid thing to do" is represented by varying clicks to the one who strayed and has returned and "I'm going to teach you a lesson" is a rapid chock, chock. "Hey, this is good to eat – am I happy!" is highly pitched and excited clicks and "Oh, what a lovely morning to be out" is a high pitched click with a slightly lower click repeated. "Okay, I'm going to bed now" is a little trilly purr and "I really do want the stag of my dreams but he's not here" a loud 'quack' call, virtually like a duck.

A broody turkey also talks to pipping eggs, constantly replies to the cheeps of poults as they hatch, communicates throughout the day when they are young and continues to do so even when they are quite grown up. She is probably saying "It's alright, I'm here" or "I'm your mother. Listen to what I'm saying!"

Should your neighbours be quite happy with the chattering and gobbling of the turkeys, then you will need to win them over in another way as well. If other animals are kept on the premises you must already realise how difficult it is to get away. They need attention

Hen turkeys can express themselves, loudly, through many different calls.

365 days a year, so thought has to be given as to who would look after the turkeys if you wanted to go on holiday. It is in no respect like taking a dog to the boarding kennels but, even if this were possible, your turkeys would certainly be happier in their own familiar environment, not to mention the additional disease risk and the stress of moving them.

Care is called for when introducing turkeys onto premises with other animals. Here a pet turkey sits contendedly not far from a pet rabbit.

A responsible neighbour who is willing to look after them well should be cherished but you can really only depend on voluntary help if there are just a few turkeys that don't take up too much time. A good-sized flock or a whole range of breeding pens calls for more organised commitment. Expect to take time to find the right person to help out and be prepared to pay the going hourly rate. That way they are less likely to think of it as a chore, will do the duty methodically and will look upon it as an occasional part-time job, thereby allowing you to count on their services again.

Introducing turkeys onto premises with other animals also calls for care during the initial integration unless they are to be given separate housing and penning of their own. You will certainly need to isolate the new birds for a fortnight as a disease precaution. Your turkey or turkeys may also never have seen a dog, cat or a cockerel before and, likewise, a large dog or even a small terrier might think that these are the best presents they've been given in ages. The last thing you need is for a dog to terrify the turkeys by barking or jumping at them or worse still, thinking that this is supper on legs. If frightened they could easily fly off or at least make a run for it and become immensely stressed. When placed in a new environment turkeys, just like cats and dogs, need to be housed for a week or ideally a fortnight, where they can see the outside world, so that they learn that this is their new home. Also, turkeys to be kept as pets or companions in the garden should be separated in this way so that they can be seen but not touched by the family's other animals until they all get to know one another. To say trust one another is difficult because I would say never leave animals together where an incident could possibly occur unless you are present. Genuine respect between all animals concerned does take a long time to build and it is unwise to take even minimal risks during the process!

Then there is the question of how long you expect to be looking after your turkeys. Those reared for meat will obviously have a limited lifespan but if kept to live could be with you for quite a while. The life expectancy of a standard turkey is seven to nine years and, although it is exceptional, I have known some turkeys to live considerably longer. Commercial birds are bred to grow to a certain weight at a specific age (in months) and will then be despatched, so if keeping these longer than that period diet and exercise need to be addressed but even they can easily live for five or six years. So under normal circumstances and if they enjoy good health, expect a turkey to live considerably longer than a hamster, a guinea pig or a gerbil. The commitment will undeniably be a long term one.

Some days will be very sad, for example when a particular turkey dies or has to be put down. These birds are very charismatic and tame ones will certainly bond with you. It is easier not to become too attached to turkeys in a flock which you know will be destined for the table. Yet even this can be hard and you will need to be very resolute when the time comes for despatching them.

One or two turkeys could quickly expand into a flock.

Of course, the cost of keeping turkeys must also be taken into consideration. A pet or two will not add up to much financially but, once that number increases to a small flock, you will have the equivalent feed and litter costs together with ongoing veterinary bills and these are of course in addition to the set up costs of housing, penning, equipment, birds and also marketing expenses and preparation costs if you are selling meat birds that are ready for the oven.

Once you become a turkey owner you must be prepared to watch for predators and vermin. If you don't think there are foxes in the area, you will discover that there are once you keep turkeys. Many are the times I've heard people say that they've lost a hen turkey to the fox as a result of having allowed her to sit on some eggs under the hedge simply because they didn't think they had foxes. Never allow a hen turkey to sit on a clutch of eggs in the open because she will end up as fox fodder. Even if the premises are surrounded by electric fencing that is in good working order, this is a very risky thing to do. You must be prepared to put the turkeys in their housing every night and to check on them at regular intervals throughout the day. You will certainly regret the one night you were late home or were too busy that evening to do the turkeys, because the chances are there will be a sorry scene in the morning. It is not simply a case of the very evening I didn't shut them in the fox came; the fox probably comes most nights but on that particular occasion he found what he wanted.

Then we come to rodents! Rats and mice will, over time, be attracted to comfortable housing where food is readily available, so a tough approach to small furry creatures will be needed to keep on top of the situation. Rodents can spread disease, damage equipment by chewing and defecating on it, eat any feed that is left uncovered and cause a stench if they become too numerous, so it is imperative to eradicate them. This can be done through a professional pest control company initially baiting and then returning to check, usually on a two monthly basis, or by baiting yourself. However, if you undertake this task it must be done efficiently and regularly with the health and safety of humans, animals and wildlife in mind because rodenticides are very poisonous. Remember also that there will be dead bodies to be disposed of after a successful baiting.

If the rodents haven't put you off then maybe the weather will. Looking after turkeys in the late spring, summer and autumn can be idyllic. On beautiful sunny days it is a pleasure to be outside but unfortunately the UK can be very wet, windy, cold and miserable in the winter but the birds will still need to be seen to if you have turkeys all year. They may well be under cover but unless they are right next to your house then carrying buckets of feed whilst battling against a gale with the rain in your face is no joke. There could well have been a hard frost

Looking after your flock in good weather is idyllic.

overnight and the locks won't work on the barn door, or the outside tap is frozen and you have to struggle back to the house to get fresh water. This is all part of everyday life when the weather is harsh. The routine of attending to the turkeys is also governed by the calendar with dark mornings in deepest winter and not much daylight in the afternoons. This is one of the reasons why it is sensible to have them housed over the winter period as it is much easier to keep them safe if you cannot be home to see to them by the time the light begins to fail.

Turkeys will instinctively go for the highest perch.

Talking of which, it is always best to make sure you have sufficient time in which to complete the task of shutting the turkeys up for the night, for you never know what might crop up and how long it will take to resolve! I will relate an experience I had one winter afternoon. It was dusk and I was just checking six four-month old Bourbon Red turkeys in their shed when one of the young hens decided to make a dash for it and escape outside. As the light was fading fast her instinct was to get high, so she flew onto the dyke (dry stone wall) behind the shed and as I approached her she shot up into the sycamore tree which grows alongside. Not content at being on a low branch she jumped onto the next and then the next until she was well out of reach of any pole or stick I had, even if I joined them together.

I was not best pleased at this because with the light almost gone and my supper time fast approaching, the last thing I wanted was another challenge in my day. To make matters worse I could hear not one but two vixens calling from different parts of the surrounding countryside. This always sends a chill down my spine, especially if some of the birds are not yet locked up. I had to get her down. There was no other option. If I had left her out I felt sure that she would have been taken before I was up again.

By now the turkey was perched way out on a side branch, almost at the top of the tree. I looked at the wide, strong tree trunk and lower branches but it took only seconds to rid myself of the notion that I might climb up, with the intention of getting close enough to poke her with a long pole. However long it was going to take me I simply had to get her down though. Then I started to think laterally. Fetching a torch and picking up an 8ft batten I went below the turkey and pretended to be a fox! Alright, I know foxes don't have torches or sticks but I was thinking of the distraction technique. I truly hoped that no-one from the cottages nearby could hear or see me because they would have immediately thought that the secluded location was doing me no good at all! I shone the bright beam of the torch onto the turkey whilst calling at it and hitting lower branches to make them sway. I kept this up until I was beginning to go slightly giddy myself but then I noticed that success was within my reach. After about 15 minutes in the treetops she was beginning to get a little disorientated. Her wings had started to open slightly, then her head moved forward then back again and her feet had begun to try to grip other branches.

After another minute or so she took to the air. Although guided by my torchlight she flew down rather guardedly into the middle of the lawn. I switched off the torch and drove her back to the wall. Luckily she had white wing feathers and it is amazing what you can see in the dark when the need arises. I then gathered her up and felt a massive sigh of relief as I returned her to her friends in the shed where at last I could be sure she was safe again.

This is by no means a case of 'don't do this at home' but rather a case of 'I hope you don't have to do this at home.' It is simply a cautionary tale to let you know what can happen on a daily basis and how turkeys do have an inbuilt instinct to roost high, especially when you least want them to. Apart from the threat of foxes, we had, earlier in the day, experienced a great storm together with gale force winds. These had died down by the time the turkey flew up into the tree but if they had returned she would never have stood a chance because force seven to eight gusts would have blown her into the neighbouring sheep pasture or even into the woods which is not something I wanted to think about as I went to bed. So instead I lay my head on the pillow with the more stoic 'all's well that ends well.'

Hopefully what you have just read hasn't dissuaded you from keeping turkeys but if it has then the chapter will have been worthwhile because you may have been saved a lot of cash, time, effort and heartache.

Chapter Four | Location, Location, Location

Providing good housing is an essential part of the preparation and your eventual choices will certainly play a large part in making any turkey project successful or otherwise.

Housing:

- Provides protection against predators, especially when the turkeys are shut in at night
- Provides the turkeys with shelter from the wind and rain
- Provides a safe place for the turkeys to sleep
- Provides an area to lay eggs, with nestboxes or a secluded area in the building
- Provides complete accommodation for rearing if free range is not an option
- Provides safety if the turkeys are required by law to be housed, for example in the event of a notifiable disease outbreak in the area

If housing a pet bird, a trio or half a dozen turkeys throughout the year, an 8ft x 6ft shed will adequately serve the purpose. This will be quite sufficient to overnight the turkeys and even house them throughout the day on occasions when the weather is too inclement to let them out. A 6ft x 4ft shed will overnight six turkeys that are being reared for the table but they will need to be outside during the day. If you are buying a new shed do go for the best quality possible, because this will last longer, particularly if given a wood preservative and regular maintenance. Placed on large runners (4 inch square stakes are ideal) the floor will be raised from the ground and remain free from damp. It will also allow space to safely put any rodenticide in a box underneath the shed for vermin control should it be needed. In areas where wind is a problem it is better to secure each corner of the shed with strong stakes knocked into the ground and

If you are buying a new shed do go for the best quality possible.

then nail or screw the shed to these from the inside. Place battens across the roof to help secure the felt. This will certainly help to prevent it being lifted off in bad weather. Ideally the felt should be the heavier mineral felt because the thin felt often supplied with garden sheds will not be sufficiently long lasting and can tear during gales or even rip if the turkeys fly onto it.

Good ventilation is essential for healthy turkeys and to provide this you can either adapt the window area or keep the polythene covered window for light and cut out another area about 2ft x 3ft on the opposite side to the prevailing winds and cover it with small mesh wire netting, doubly securing the edges with battens. This will allow plenty of air to circulate whilst keeping predators out. If the shed is not positioned in a sheltered area then it is a good idea to make a canopy projecting down from the top of the opening with side panels to prevent any driving rain getting inside. Any openings should be made as high as possible in the shed so that draughts do not affect the turkeys. In some buildings, especially those made of steel and tin, condensation can occur creating a damp atmosphere and damp litter. During very cold nights frost can cling to the inside of the roof and as the temperature rises during the day this drips off so plenty of air is needed to circulate and dry out any moisture.

Although it is always a good idea to give the birds as much space as possible, if they are outside free ranging during the day the overnight accommodation, e.g. a 6ft x 4ft shed for six turkeys, will be for sleeping only and will not be their only environment.

New housing might not be needed because there could well be a building on the property already that could be customised. Looking at this option should be a priority if you are considering rearing birds for the table because once you begin to spend large amounts of money on housing it will take longer for any return to be made. It is amazing what can be done with any building, so long as it has ventilation, is not in disrepair, has a predator proof door and window/s and is vermin proof as well, although in the case of the latter you will certainly need to eradicate any vermin if they are found on the premises. Unless a building is brand new, always give it a good wash down with disinfectant to clean it thoroughly before putting any birds in. If it is made of stone or brick then a good coating of white emulsion inside, once it has been disinfected, will make it look smarter and lighter. Then, with a perch or perches and clean shavings or straw, the dwelling should make an ideal turkey house.

Perches

Your turkeys will certainly appreciate perches because they do like to get off the ground at night and either a pole about 2 inches in circumference or a stake that has been bevelled at a height approximately 2 to 2½ ft off the floor will be suitable. In a 6ft by 4ft shed, which can accommodate six meat turkeys overnight, erect two perches at a height of about 2ft. Although turkeys are able to fly much higher than this, in a small shed they

Aim to get the perches level to keep bullying at bay

would not have sufficient room in which to fly down safely without landing heavily. In a vast barn they could perch fairly high up because of the space available to get down but even then it is best not to encourage high perching because birds can injure themselves when descending causing lameness or broken bones, especially in males.

A group of free-standing perches could be made for a small flock of turkeys in a larger house and these would be very useful if permanent fixtures are not required. These can be made by constructing two stout frames 4ft by 10ft, then connecting them at each corner with 3 inch by 3 inch stakes 2ft high so that the frames are parallel with each other. Then secure five 2 inch by 2 inch poles 4ft long on top of the frame. The end poles will fit on top of the existing frame with the three remaining poles each 2½ft from those and each other. This would cater for about fifteen perching turkeys if they all got on with one another. Perches on a single level (as opposed to perches that are built gradually ascending an A-frame) are better for keeping the peace! Instinctively turkeys like to get as high as possible and if only a few can get on to the top perch it can provoke a hierarchy that could eventually result in bullying. If they are level then this is less likely to happen. On the floor of turkey housing I prefer to use shavings because I find they stay drier longer than straw and are less prone to any mustiness but obviously you will need to take into account what is best for you and the availability of either product.

Nestboxes

Breeder females will need to have something in which to encourage them to lay their eggs. This will lessen the possibility of birds laying outside, where eggs can get dirty or even be taken by

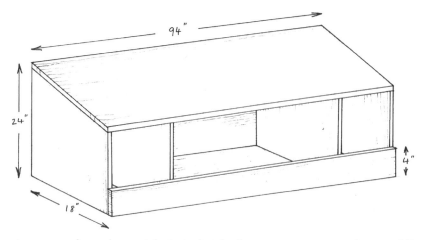

A suggested nestbox with 2 individual compartments and a middle communal area.

predators such as carrion crows. A nestbox should allow plenty of room for a female turkey to shift around and sit in comfort. A plywood box about 15 inches by 18 inches with two sides 2ft high, a roof and 4 inch litter retaining boards at each end should be quite suitable. Obviously, if more than one turkey is to be provided for then either a longer box or more boxes will be needed. A nestbox 5ft long should accommodate ten hens. I hesitate to put too much emphasis on a specific pattern for the ideal nestbox because someone could spend a lot of time and effort in building one, only to have the birds snub it completely, which could be very disheartening.

Hen turkeys are just looking for somewhere quiet and secluded to lay their eggs and this is what you should aim to provide for them. In one of my turkey pens there is a large old tree that was felled because it was rotten inside. Over the years the rotten wood has worn away and left a massive hole and the turkeys tend to ignore the nestbox in the house, preferring to disappear into the tree trunk to lay their eggs. At least I know where to find them and so far the crows haven't discovered this egg hideout yet. One of the cheapest nestboxes you could provide is a large old tyre in a corner of the house. The inside ring of the tyre needs to be stuffed with straw so that no eggs can fall into it and get lost but once this is done and a good delve of straw or shavings is placed in the middle it does make a good nest. A tea-chest on its side facing a corner of the

A large old tyre is one of the cheapest nestboxes.

house or even a large bottom drawer of a chest of drawers can be taken to quite readily. If the turkey house is a good size, an old door placed on its side, propped against the wall will entice them behind it. Do make sure, though, that if you do provide anything like this that it is securely fastened and cannot fall down on any unsuspecting turkey.

When several turkeys use the same nesting area it is possible for eggs to get broken and if this happens it is crucial that it is cleaned out as soon as possible. The last thing you want to happen is for the turkeys to get a taste for egg and to start eating them, so thoroughly remove all traces of mess and replace with clean shavings or straw. Hay is not recommended because of the possibility it may contain fungal spores. Throughout the laying season the boxes should be checked whenever possible because if the weather is very hot and birds overcrowd the nestbox then suffocation could occur. Also, when the turkeys go broody they can pack themselves into nestboxes like sardines, sitting tight and refusing to budge even if other birds are on top of them.

Fencing

To allow turkeys to roam outside you will need some form of fencing. For permanent fencing, 6ft high 2 inch mesh is usually used for turkeys because 4ft high chicken mesh is not tall enough and turkeys will easily hop over this, especially if there is someone next door that they would rather be with. You can clip their wings but the females are quite adept at flapping their wings and clambering up wire with their feet. If you don't have a vast area to surround then 6ft chain link fencing is certainly worth considering as, although more expensive, it will be stronger and will last longer.

Ordinary wire fencing must be strenthened with an extra layer of mesh.

When a row of pens is needed to separate different varieties and stag turkeys will be on either side, ordinary wire mesh fencing must be strengthened along the lower half of the fence. This can be done by running a layer of smaller mesh wire about 3ft high all the way along the bottom of the taller fencing. Stags will fight through the wire, especially during the early part of the mating season and can easily break the wire and even sever it completely along the bottom. The second layer of wire does tend to prevent damage in this way and the smaller mesh means the birds are less likely to actually make contact if they do try to fight. Alternatively, gauze netting can be fixed in the same way and this makes it less obvious for the birds to see each other.

Ideally any perimeter fencing should be buried into the ground and run about 2½ft out from the fence, which will take another layer of wire mesh to complete. This can then be re-covered by soil and should prevent foxes from digging under the wire as they don't usually start digging beyond this distance from the fence. If you are in an area where foxes abound, it might be worth installing electric wires similar to those used for the protection of pheasant pens, which run along the bottom of the fencing.

Fixed pen wire netting and staking can be rather expensive and an alternative for free range turkeys would be electric fence netting. This serves two purposes as it contains the turkeys and keeps foxes out. It will, however, still be prudent to house the birds at night. A fox attack is a most horrendous sight and could devastate a small flock and any profit you had in mind. I cannot emphasise enough that even though they are large, adult turkeys are by no means fox-proof. Even during the daytime when the birds are out, the challenge will be to keep the fencing in good working order and this will mean checking for any possible short-circuits etc. on a daily basis.

Electric netting is suitable for a single flock of a hundred birds on a small area but for a larger area catering for thousands of turkeys nine-line wires are more appropriate. Electric netting comes in 50 metre lengths and you should expect to pay around £70 a length. An energiser is about £100 and an earth stake £5 plus VAT. The stocking rate for conventionally reared free range turkeys is around five hundred per acre, so fifty birds in your first year could be reared on a reasonably small piece of land. Any electric fencing, if maintained properly, could be added to the following year if you chose to increase the number of turkeys kept.

One big advantage of electric fencing is that it can be moved around and therefore, if you have the space, the turkeys can be moved to fresh grazing as needed. This helps to prevent the build up of disease and keeps the land healthier as well as the turkeys. Bear in mind, though, that you will need to drive the turkeys back to their housing at night unless the fencing can be moved around the house or leading to the house. Turkeys are very good at being driven just so long as you do it quietly and slowly so they are not panicked. They do get used to a routine and most will put themselves away but there are always a few that want to stay up late! You need to usher these in then make absolutely sure that the door is securely shut.

14 week old poults: Bourbon Red, Blue, Narragansett, Norfolk Black and Slate.

Stocking rates

There are set stocking rates for keeping turkeys commercially; primarily for the purpose of animal welfare and to inform consumers of how the birds were reared when marketing them.

Extensively kept indoors (barn reared)

The term may only be used where the stocking rate per square metre of floor space does not exceed 25kgs of live weight for turkeys and the birds are slaughtered at seventy days or later.

Free range

This term may only be used where the stocking rate is as for barn reared in the house with the birds having, during at least half their lifetime, continuous daytime access to open-air runs comprising an area mainly covered by vegetation of not less than 4 square metres per turkey.

Traditional free range

This term may only be used where the indoor stocking rate per square metre does not exceed 10 poults up to the age of seven weeks, 6.25 above that age but not more than 35kg live weight. The total usable area of poultry houses at any single production site does not exceed 1,600 square metres and each poultry house does not contain more than 2,500 turkeys. The poultry house is provided with pop holes of a combined length at least equal to 4 metres per 100 square metres surface of the house. There is continuous day-time access to open-air runs at least from the age of 8 weeks in the case of turkeys. Open-air runs comprise an area mainly covered by vegetation amounting to at least 6 square metres per turkey. The turkeys being fattened are of a strain recognised as being slow growing, the feed formula used in the fattening stage contains at least 70% cereals and the minimum age at slaughter is 140 days.

Free range (total freedom)

The use of this term requires the stocking density to be as for Traditional free range, except that the birds will have continuous day-time access to open-air runs of unlimited area.

Chapter Five | You are what you Eat

To look after turkeys there are a number of items of equipment that will be needed and the most basic of these are feeders and drinkers.

Day-old poults up to three or four weeks need only have a shallow utensil for the turkey starter crumbs. A plastic tray with a low rim is ideal as the poults can easily get to the crumbs. Once the dish is soiled it can be disposed of and replaced. Even the reverse side of a plastic feeder base is useful and this way the poults will get used to the coloured feeder base, so when it is turned the correct way up with the plastic feed fount on top they will already be used to the coloured tray of feed. Small galvanised troughs are also available which are equally suitable for young poults.

Small plastic founts with narrow rims make ideal drinkers for poults. These are specially designed for very young birds, where they can drink efficiently but not get wet. As fresh water is so important to young poults it is better if they have access to more than one drinker. Never give poults a large dish of water that they can walk into as they will get wet, chill and then die, even with a heat-lamp nearby. Whichever feeders and drinkers you use they must be immaculately clean and thoroughly disinfected before being used by poults.

Poult feeders and drinkers displayed on an anti-litter stand.

Growing poults have similar utensils but these are larger. It is important to change the size of feeding and drinking equipment in line with the growth of the poults or they will not be eating or drinking sufficient quantities for their nutritional requirements. To help keep litter from drinkers and feeders, set them on bricks, wire stands or circular plastic stands. This enables the poults to get to the feed and water but helps to keep them free of shavings. Feeders and drinkers will need to be tidied up or emptied and replenished throughout the day because of contamination; poults are not particular where they defecate and you don't want any possible bacteria accumulation in the drinking water. If bricks or stands are not used, place a piece of board on the ground for the utensils but clear away any soiled feed on the ground or wet shavings daily to prevent the build up of stale feed and bacteria.

A selection of large galvanised feeders or their plastic equilivants

There are several feeders suitable for adult turkeys. Large galvanised turkey feeders can be hung at chest height so that the birds feed from the wide rim and feed is kept at a distance from the floor. These are quite heavy pieces of equipment, especially when full of feed, and they need something strong to hang them from. There are plastic versions which are cheaper and lighter. Troughs are easy to use but need to be positioned carefully because the turkeys can knock them over and the last thing you want is feed in the litter, much of which will be wasted. Stabilising the trough with bricks can help. Outside troughs have a protected cover along the top to prevent the weather from soiling the feed, however, to protect turkeys from possible disease risks from wild birds, keepers are encouraged to feed them inside or at least away from wild birds. In free-range systems this can be a little difficult but if the turkeys get used to being fed inside their housing this will help to lessen any wild bird contact.

A range of drinkers are available from poult to adults.

When drinking an adult turkey needs to get half of its beak into water to drink properly, so nothing too shallow is adequate. Galvanised bucket drinkers are suitable for growing poults and turkey hens but stags might find them more difficult as they would have to drink at an angle. Also, as the bucket does not come apart, it would need to be cleaned by steeping it in disinfectant or Milton steriliser. Good hygiene is so important that you are better off with something that you know you will and can clean quickly, rather than something that may look more hygienic but takes great effort to sterilise. The largest of the water fount drinkers are suitable for turkeys but all my adult birds drink from ordinary plastic buckets. These are cheap, hold plenty of water and are easy to clean. Keep a scrubbing brush and some disinfectant near the water-tap and then when you get fresh water – which should be every day – quickly scrub round the inside of the bucket and rinse it out before refilling. This takes up very little time but could pay dividends by preventing the birds from picking up unwanted organisms from the drinker. Even if a bucket looks clean, it is amazing how quickly it can get grimy and this will harbour bacteria. Then, once a week, thoroughly disinfect it as well. One vital point though if using a bucket for drinking purposes.

Feeders can be hung up rather than left on the floor. This limits dirt getting in the feed.

Always make sure the handle is down below the lip of the bucket. Surprising as it may seem, it has been known for a bird to get its head stuck underneath the handle and drown in the bucket of water.

A correct feeding programme is vitally important for the development of turkeys.

Feeding

A correct feeding programme is vitally important for the development and good health of turkeys. They become large, active, big boned birds and rely on you, their owner, to keep them well fed and fit.

The good news is that you have support in doing this because there are proprietary feeds for specific species such as turkeys that cover the age range from day-old to adult. It is in the manufacturer's interest to get formulations correct because if there was a problem they would soon have to stop production or at least address it.

Very large turkey producers have resources for bulk storage of feed but smaller producers and certainly those with less than hundred turkeys would probably find feed in bagged form more convenient. Even if you happen to have a large storage facility you must remember that pellet feed has a limited life and the last thing you want is for it to be sitting in a silo past its sell by date

Three hens practice synchronised insect hunting.

and beginning to go mouldy. Freshly made up pellet feed has a shelf life of about three months, so aim to buy or order feed from your agricultural merchant that will easily be used up before its goes stale.

The amount of feed needed will depend on whether the turkeys are totally housed or have access to vegetation during the day. Working on rough guidelines a small double-cupped handful of feed per adult turkey in the morning and a single cupped handful of wheat in the afternoon is generally sufficient. However, I am not going to even attempt to list a consumption rate because it will not be the same for all situations and I don't want to give figures that people adhere to only to later find that they are inaccurate and the turkeys are being affected. It is much better to give an amount that you think reasonable and then add to it if it is disappearing in minutes, or reduce it if there is feed left in the trough at the end of the day. Handling the turkeys is one of the best ways of telling if a bird is 'doing well' and putting on weight or if it perhaps feels underweight. Remember though, a lack of weight could also mean a health problem and not just one of inappropriate feed quantities.

Most turkey feed comes in 20kg bags and before loading up your purchases do make sure that you read the label on the bag just to make sure that you have the correct feed. Often, a manufacturer's range of bagged feed can look similar in pattern and colour and the label may be the only distinguishing mark between different feeds, even feeds for different species. So do check! Once you have the feed it should be stored in a cool dry place away from any rodents or wild birds. Ideally the feed should be emptied out of the bags and put in a rodent free container because paper bags are subject to being nibbled, are susceptible to damp and you certainly don't want contamination of any sort seeping through onto the feed. There is quite a range of feed storage containers on the market and they are excellent. The size of storage container will very much depend on the number of turkeys you will be providing for. This may seem obvious but what you don't want to do is have storage capacity that is too large so that you are tempted to buy more bags than you need and end up with feed at the bottom of the container going stale. Purpose built storage containers are made in galvanised steel and generally come with anything from one compartment up to four. They are smart, rodent proof and ideal for the job. Expect to pay anything from £40 to £300.

If you keep around fifty turkeys then plastic or galvanised dustbins would also do the job adequately. Plastic bins are not totally rodent free but you are going to be keeping them under control! They are certainly much cheaper, coming in at under £10, and an ordinary dustbin itself will hold two bags of feed. A plastic scoop will help you to fill buckets of feed much quicker and this will cost between £3 and £4. Separate storage containers will be needed for the different range of pellets and wheat. Do make sure that they are clearly marked up.

A group of turkeys dine out on nettles.

The formulations of turkey feed will consist of protein, carbohydrates, oils, minerals and vitamins. Proteins are necessary for growth, body maintenance and reproduction. Turkeys require a high protein content in their feed, more so than chickens. Carbohydrates are divided into those that are soluble and those that are insoluble. Soluble carbohydrates are broken down into sugars and these provide energy, with any excess sugars being stored as fat. Insoluble carbohydrates are the fibre content. These are not nutritional but assist in making the feed more palatable. This is important because if the birds do not like the look or feel of the feed they will not eat sufficiently or sometimes at all. Oil in feed is broken down by the digestive juices into glycerine and fatty acids which also produce energy. Minerals are required for the growth and maintenance of the bones, egg shell, tissue and muscles. There will be some reference to minerals on feed bags such as copper but normally they are listed as the 'ash' percentage. A range of vitamins are found in turkey feed formulations and the highest quantity is usually that of Vitamin A. This is essential for good growth and a deficiency will lower the bird's capacity for dealing with the challenge of diseases.

The ingredients will include wheat, different forms of soya, maize germ and limestone but can vary according to availability of the ingredients at the time and different manufacturers' formulations.

Guide to turkey feed

Always order the feed you require in advance so that it is available when you need it.

Turkey Starter Crumbs

Turkey starter crumbs are for day-old poults through until they are about five weeks old. They are essential for good development and contain 26-27% protein which is a higher protein content than chick crumbs. Chick crumbs should certainly not be given as not only do they not contain sufficient protein but some formulations contain the coccidiostat salinomycin which could kill the poults. Poults should be given turkey starter crumbs ad lib and although feed should not be allowed to build up around the feeder and become stale, young poults should never be left without feed and should therefore be checked at regular intervals.

Turkey Rearer Pellets

When the poults are around four to five weeks old begin to mix rearer pellets into the turkey starter crumbs and slowly wean them off the crumbs. Rearer pellets are a small pellet formulation with 24% protein that is given between the ages of five to eight weeks. Rearer pellets should be given ad lib.

Turkey Grower Pellets

Turkey grower pellets contain 21% protein and are added to the rearer diet at around eight weeks so that by the time the poults are nine weeks old they are on the grower ration only. Some turkey keepers mix the starter crumbs with grower pellets for about a fortnight, thus moving directly from starter to grower. Poults have been seen to adapt to this change without any noticeable effect, however, a gradual decline in protein would certainly help to maintain a consistency of development. If poults are housed during this stage of development there should always be plenty of feed available. Should they be running outside as well they will be supplementing their diet with vegetation.

Turkey Finisher Pellets

Poults being grown on for table birds will move to a finisher ration anytime between the ages of twelve to sixteen weeks. A finisher is a fattening ration that will put weight onto the birds and help to 'finish' the texture of the meat. The protein level is around 16%.

Turkey Breeder Pellets

Turkeys that are not being kept for the table move from a grower to a breeder ration which usually contains around 15% protein. This feed contains added vitamins and calcium to prepare the birds for egg production. It is a well balanced ration suitable for all adult turkeys including pets.

Pellets are fed in the morning as they are easily digestible and it is important that the birds have a good nutritional diet at the start of the day.

Grain

When poults are twelve weeks old they can be introduced to grain. This is normally in the form of wheat. It is not given before this age because the digestive system will not have developed sufficiently to be able to deal with it. Just give a small amount at first and do so in the afternoon.

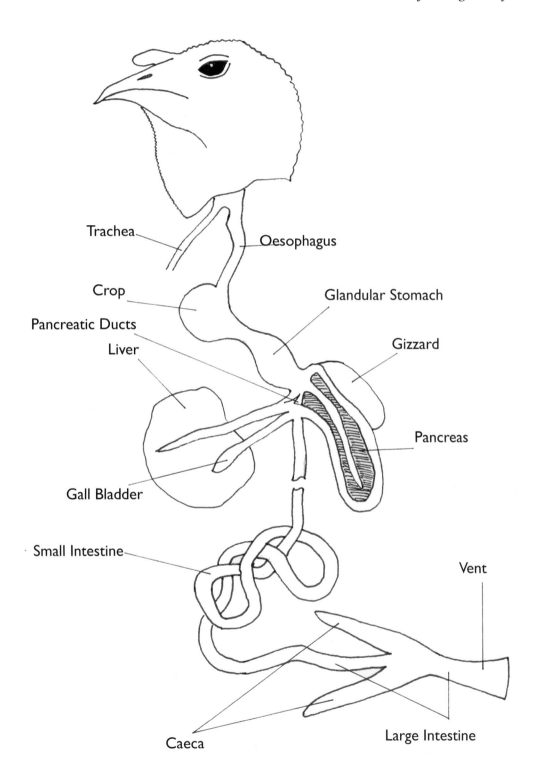

Illustration of the digestive system.

Trachea

Oesophagus

Crop

Glandular Stomach

Pancreatic Ducts

Liver

Gizzard

Pancreas

Gall Bladder

Small Intestine

Vent

Caeca

Large Intestine

Grain should always be the second feed of the day because it is less nutritious than the formulated pellet feed. Also, grain stays in the crop longer so will help to keep the birds content overnight.

Cut maize can also be given in small amounts during the winter months. It is not recommended for use in the summer though as it is a warming feed. Naked oats can also be given to turkeys and this is a grain often used for commercial birds as it gives a good finish to the meat.

Grit

For turkeys to be able to make the best use of feed in their digestive system they will need to have a supply of grit. This helps to grind roughage in the gizzard and can actually lead to a healthier bird. Very fine chick grit can be given to poults as early as 3-4 days old. Just mix a little in with the starter crumbs or put some in a shallow dish where they can scratch about and peck at it. As the poults develop they graduate to mixed poultry grit. This may contain small pieces of oyster shell but never give oyster shell alone as this is far too smooth and can lead to impaction and even death over time. Access to grit is essential for turkeys that are constantly housed but even free range birds will readily use it. Place a small heap of grit in a container either somewhere in the outside pen, near the feed trough or even in the feed trough and do this on a monthly basis. If you ever have a post mortem done on a turkey do have a look at the inside of the gizzard and you will see a collection of tiny stones and the importance of supplementing grit will become very clear.

Greenery

Turkeys love to graze and will do so as soon as they are let out in the morning. Free range turkeys should have adequate vegetation in their penning area as this plays a vital role in providing a good all-round diet. Short grass is more beneficial and safer than long grass which could impact the crop. Lawn or hedge trimmings should never be given to turkeys. Wilting grass and leaves quickly go mouldy and these can ferment in the crop and cause toxicity problems.

Whilst outside turkeys will also go for insects, especially in the late summer and early autumn when they are plentiful. Crane flies are a favourite but it might also be that they enjoy playing the game of catching them. Berries and seeds will also be eaten with gusto.

To keep turkeys happy whilst being housed, hang up some greenery in the form of cabbages, brussels sprout tops or kale. These will not only give the birds something to do and relieve any boredom but will also be improving the diet.

Treats

Sunflower seeds certainly get any turkey's vote! They love them. Do not give them too many. A handful mixed amongst a bucket of wheat is sufficient because they are quite fattening but the oil certainly helps with feather conditioning. Apples, plums, grapes, fresh corn on the cob, or even tinned corn can be fed to turkeys as little treats. Some birds I know also like tiny pieces of granary bread and raisins.

What to avoid

If turkeys have access to the garden or any wooded areas be aware of poisonous plants. Usually birds have an inbuilt sense when it comes to what not to eat but young turkeys do like to experiment and will walk around pecking at this and that as they pass by it.

Make sure the land your turkey will be grazing on is free from poisonous plants

Plants that are definitely poisonous are aconitum, yew, ragwort, foxglove, hellebore, hemlock, poison ivy, black bryony, cherry laurel, clematis, dropwort, black & deadly nightshade, laburnum seeds, potato sprouts and potatoes that have been unearthed and turned green, some irises, castor bean, St. John's wort, vetch, rapeseed, rhododendron, sweet pea, corn cockle, henbane and various fungi.

Avoid any stale or mouldy feed as this is asking for problems. Also, make sure there are no stale pieces of feed stuck in the corners of feeders, which should be kept clean and disinfected on a regular basis. Try to prevent access to any stale water and most certainly any blue-green algae. If turkeys drink from stagnant water they do risk being affected by botulism. The bacteria clostridium botulinum flourishes in hot weather when water levels are low and this can produce toxicity problems in birds.

Water

No chapter about feed would be complete without highlighting the importance of water. Fresh water should be provided on a daily basis and is essential for the health and welfare of turkeys, especially poults, as they can develop gut problems and even die of water starvation if they do not take in sufficient liquid.

Water consumption should generally, as a proportion, be twice as much as the feed intake but this varies greatly according to the age of the birds, the weather, the temperature and their environment. Day-olds will need small narrow lipped fount chick drinkers. More drinkers will be needed the more poults you have and these will need to be checked every hour or so to gauge how much water they actually need and to refresh the water. Poults have very little concept of hygiene so the drinker should be thoroughly cleaned and fresh water given regularly to prevent any contamination. Drinkers stood on trays also help to prevent litter from getting into the water.

Growing poults will need larger drinkers and as they grow the daily intake of water will increase. Adult turkeys should have access to plenty of water and this will need to be changed several times a day in very hot weather. Drinking cold water will help to keep birds cool but if it is left to become warm in high temperatures it can become stale with a possible bacteria risk.

Feed for sick turkeys

If a turkey is off its feed and noticeably not eating then investigation is needed to see what the problem is. When this happens and even whilst medication is being given, it is essential to get sustenance into the bird but liquid is far more important than feed at this stage. A turkey will decline rapidly if its liquid intake is poor.

A turkey may drink a little if you gently push its head down so that the beak goes into a bowl of fresh water. This should not in itself stress the bird too much. Often it may react by supping up some water to drink. If this doesn't work then an alternative is to syringe a little water down its throat (about 1ml at a time) containing some form of supplement, even glucose if nothing else is readily available. Syringes can easily be obtained from a veterinary practice and other outlets. A 2ml syringe is ideal for this purpose. The vital thing to beware of is not to syringe water down the windpipe which is at the front portion of the throat. This can be avoided by pointing down the back of the throat, or even attaching a small piece of narrow plastic tubing to the syringe so that the liquid definitely heads towards the crop.

There are various supplements made by animal health companies that can be added to your turkeys' drinking water and these are readily available via advertisements in poultry and smallholder magazines, agricultural merchants, poultry equipment businesses and veterinary practices. They are normally in liquid form and contain vitamins, trace elements, essential amino acids, essential fatty acids, electrolytes and even nucleotides - the natural building blocks of DNA and RNA, which help with development and immunity to disease.

These supplements are extremely useful in assisting recovery from disease, stress, during a diet change, the moult, following the natural incubation period for a broody, following an outing to a show, transportation and rehousing.

Ensuring that a turkey continues to receive feed is a little more difficult. However, a special recipe has been devised for sick turkeys and according to a poultry nutritionist it is full of beneficial ingredients. The recipe is as follows:

1 tablespoon Soya mince (dried)	1 teaspoon Pearl barley
1 tablespoon Sunflower seed hearts	1 teaspoon Bulgar wheat
1 tablespoon Pumpkin seeds	2-3 halves Walnut
1 teaspoon Pine kernels	½ teaspoon Dandelion leaf tea
1 teaspoon Sesame seeds	(dry)

Ground the ingredients finely in a coffee bean grinder or an electric blender. Mix them with the minimum amount of warm water to form a paste which can be applied using a syringe but remember that if it is too wet the turkey is just filling up with water and won't drink any medicated water. Use either a large syringe such as those used for worming a horse or roll the paste into a very small ball and pop it down the throat. Be sure the paste ball goes right down the back of the throat and not into the windpipe. This recipe is highly palatable and the turkey will not react as though it is a nasty medicine. Administer this every two hours or so until the bird is stronger and able to feed itself.

If a turkey is sick it is essential that it continues to take in liquid and nutrients because veterinary medicines alone will be insufficient to keep the bird from deteriorating.

Keeping cool under a Medlar tree

Chapter Six | Doing What comes Naturally

Turkeys will adapt to the way in which you look after them and can become immensely tame if time and consideration is given to them. If poults are reared with plenty of human contact and gentle handling, when they are adults it will be far easier to look after them. Of course two or three turkeys will always be easier to handle and will respond more to individual attention than a flock of about fifty. The greater the number of turkeys, the more they will react to one another rather than the person looking after them but even in this situation with good husbandry the birds can be encouraged to stay calm, allowing themselves to be driven and housed if dealt with at all times in a quiet manner. This way they will get used to taking everyday occurrences in their stride and be less likely to stampede or huddle in a corner with the risk of suffocation if startled.

Well-behaved turkeys will be a joy to have around. No turkey should have to be given an anti-social behaviour order (ASBO) but just occasionally I have come across the odd rogue; most likely a stag with an enormous chip on his shoulder. Constant ill-temper may be caused by a genetic problem, not having been handled properly or being handled roughly, a lack of communication and good stockmanship from the keeper or just sheer bad luck.

Depending on how serious the misbehaviour is it might be worth trying to address the situation by increasing the amount of kindly attention the bird is given; by talking to it, handling it or holding your outstretched hand above the bird as though 'blessing' it just so that it is clear that you are a much bigger person than it and are taking control. When trying to handle and talk to such a turkey do make sure that your face is not too close to a beak or claw, both of which could cause a nasty scratch or even a tear. Never ever be tempted to 'teach it a lesson' and act aggressively towards the turkey, for that would simply be reinforcing the bad behaviour although this course of action may try your patience, especially if the bird has just flown at you with feet kicking and beak pecking.

Although I would at all times attempt to address the situation, I would never want anyone who is not used to turkeys, or any children, to run the risk of being attacked by such a bird and if the behaviour is very bad I would recommend that it be despatched. The last thing you want is for a child to be attacked, or to breed from such a bird and possibly pass on similar behavioural traits. It is also important to be aware that such aggression in front of other turkeys does not induce a settled, contented environment for the rest of the flock. I must impress though that this extreme behaviour is rare and most turkeys are much more docile. For every turkey that dramatically exhibits aggressive behaviour there will be hundreds who are impeccably behaved.

Sometimes, what is perceived as aggressive behaviour can occur in a pet turkey that has been brought up with no other turkey around. When bringing up individual birds it is still important to remember and for the turkey to realise that it is not a human; however tame it may get and even if it enjoys lots of human company. If there are other birds around, even if they are not turkeys, then it will, to some extent, identify with them but if there are no other birds present, then your behaviour and that of your children will prove to be a major influence. As a tiny poult it will scramble over you if you sit down with it and this will be fine for bonding and to encourage trust but as the poult grows the activities that it sees you partake in could affect how it behaves. If children are running around the garden kicking at a football and the turkey is in there with them, don't be surprised if it starts to jump up and kick as well. It is, after all, what it is subconsciously being 'taught' to do.

Two are always preferable to one.

There are numerous examples of individual turkeys that are kept quite happily and get on with life in a remarkably calm and well behaved way but if given the choice I do think that two turkeys are always preferable to one as they can then go about doing 'turkey' things and reacting to each other. A stag and a hen is possibly the best option but two hens will also make great friends and even two stags will be fine if brought up with each other. Even so, be prepared for the odd disagreement, especially with the stags in the early spring.

They have an inbuilt sexual need to be 'top turkey' and testosterone will become more important than friendship, at least for a while. Hen turkeys can also have 'bitchy' times and may even need to be separated for a day or two but similarly, these feelings and the unsociable behaviour will pass.

Turkey keepers should not confuse a stag 'displaying' with aggression. When a stag turkey is displaying, fluffing up all his feathers and holding his tail in a fan shape, he is not showing aggression but is trying to show himself in the best possible light to other turkeys around and if there aren't any,

Treat the stag with respect during the breeding season.

then anyone or anything that can see how splendid he looks will do.

A stag that displays constantly is a very fit, healthy and happy bird and at a show such a turkey will gladly show off all day, although he might be quite tired by the evening. When stags reach maturity, which is from about six months of age, they will also 'drum.' This action gives the impression that he is stamping up and down very rapidly on the spot, with back humped, feathers fluffed out and wings down beside him. This is not an aggressive display. It is a preparatory sexual act as well as a sign to others that he is ready to mate.

During the breeding season a few stag turkeys may become slightly threatening but this is because they feel very protective towards their hens at this very important time of the year. These stags only need to be treated with respect. The keeper should not antagonise the bird or put him or herself in a position which looks subordinate. Calmly walk around the stag and try to keep a distance so that no situation arises. If necessary, walk sideways or backwards through a gate so that you do not give the slightest provocation or encouragement for any reaction. If you do not respond to this protective behaviour it will disappear as the season goes on and the bird will normally revert to being a well adjusted turkey once the importance of reproduction is not so uppermost in his mind.

The turkey New Year begins in late December/January when the stags

A saddle should be put on the hen to prevent injury.

Hens are not restricted when wearing saddles.

begin to show more of an interest in the hens. It is then that any hens running with males should have a saddle put on. Turkey breeding saddles help to prevent the stag damaging the female whilst he is 'treading' her. So important are they to welfare that the Government department for overseeing animal welfare, the Department for Environment, Food and Rural Affairs (DEFRA) in the Turkey Welfare Code, states that "before turkey hens are naturally mated they should be fitted with strong saddles to prevent injury to the back and sides by the males." A saddle is about a breakfast plate sized piece of leather (or canvas) with a semi-circle of thicker leather strips on the upper part. The stag balances on the piece of leather and the strips are designed to catch his claws when he treads so that they do not scrape down the sides of the hen.

The saddles sit on the backs of the hens and their wings pass through straps that hold the saddle in position. It is, in fact, very similar to when I was a child and carried my school satchel on my back with each arm going through a leather strap. Both leather and canvas saddles are good but unless the canvas is quite strong and thick the male can sometimes 'ruck' it up, which of course defeats the object if he is then treading the hen's feathers and bare skin.

To put a saddle on a hen turkey, pull one of the straps right through the connecting piece of material at the front of the saddle until it is in a large loop, then gather up the hen's wing feathers and thread them through the loop. Once you have made sure that all the feathers are through, turn the turkey round and hold her against you so that her other wing is ready to be threaded through. Pull the strap back through to the other side, making the loop as large as possible, and thread the second wing through. Make sure all the feathers are cleanly through, then even up the straps so that the saddle sits comfortably on her back. She may well move around rather awkwardly for a few minutes trying to unsettle this strange object but will very soon get used to it and eventually take no notice. A saddle will not restrict the turkey at all She will still be able to

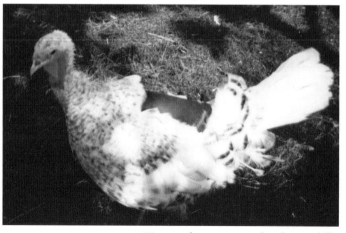

Hen turkey wearing leather saddle.

fly, jump, have dust baths and carry out other day to day turkey duties. She will preen around it but it is a good idea to check from time to time that the saddle is not rubbing and making any part of her sore and that feathers are remaining in good condition under the saddle.

It is also essential to check regularly that her feathers are not covering up any mating damage. Even with a saddle a stag can still damage the hen if she is knocked sideways and he treads her side rather than her back. If injured she may well look rather sorry for herself and hold her wings in a slightly droopy fashion.

During mating it is usually the hen that calls the tune.

Isolate her immediately, take off the saddle and investigate the extent of the wound. If it is just scratches then put some antiseptic powder or spray on her and let her recover on her own for a few days. Sometimes the damage can be more serious and may warrant a visit to the vet for stitches and an antibiotic. With isolation, treatment and some tender loving care, it is amazing how well hens can recover but be sure to have them really fit and fully saddled again before putting them back with a stag. If seriously damaged she may need the remainder of the season to recover because any new growth of skin will be tender and you don't want to run the risk of damage again in the same place, which will then take longer to heal.

When mating occurs it is usually the hen that calls the tune. She squats before the stag and if he is taking no notice she will get up, walk around him and squat again. Sometimes hens can be rejected for a while and they then become quite frustrated. It is not unusual for a hen to fall for a stag in the next pen, whereby she promptly squats as close to the netting as possible, tempting the stag next door and possibly upsetting his hens as well. Squatting is a natural action for hens at the start of the mating season. Their hormones take over and regardless of whether they are with stags or not, they will do it. Hens will also squat for the person who looks after them but with a few strokes, some kind words and some feed, they soon get over this urge. Once squatting and mating occur, eggs will follow about three to four weeks later. A successful mating will result in the hen turkey being fertile for several weeks which is why it is so important that different breeds are kept separately from one another. It only takes one illicit mating for 'gene drift' to affect what is produced, resulting in a cross-breed.

Younger stags are likely to be more fertile than the older ones, so in a breeding pen use stags that are no more than three to four years old if possible. Certainly older males will still perform but their fertility will be far less dependable. Fertility will also be affected if antibiotics have been administered because of infection, in which case time alone will sort out the problem. Hens will stay productive for longer but I would not expect too much from them once they reach five to six years of age.

The optimum time of year for fertility is from March to May, after which it begins to decline. Occasionally stags get a 'second wind' and it is possible for fertility to rise again around July. Good sunny days certainly help to bolster fertility and if it has been a cold, wet spring then an improvement in the weather often means an improvement in fertility as well. Also, it can take a stag a little while to actually tread the hens correctly, so be patient with him. If it is his first time he may even try treading her the wrong way round and I have actually seen a hen turkey dive under a stag in an effort to get him to carry out his duty properly. Eventually though, things will work out, especially if there are other turkeys that can be seen carrying out the procedure correctly.

Should the level of fertility be very important, such as in breeding pens where poults are required for meat production, then artificial insemination would be the answer. Many of the commercial flocks artificially inseminate for this reason. The intensively reared heavier turkeys are generally artificially inseminated because they are unable to mate efficiently due to their size and weight.

To carry out artificial insemination the stags need to be handled on a regular basis. They will then get used to the procedure quite quickly. The whole process needs to be thoroughly organised so that no time is wasted in catching up and preparing birds. Two people are needed, one to hold the turkey and the other to gather the semen, along with a small glass funnel and a pipette or semen straw, which must be scrupulously clean. It is probably better for the person holding the turkey to sit down so that it can be held across the lap. Gently massage the abdomen towards the vent. When the stag reacts the sex organ will protrude from the vent and the person with the funnel should press the thumb and first finger of the left hand firmly on either side of the vent so that the semen flows into the funnel. Once the stag responds there is little time in which to carry out the task but if all has worked well it is possible to collect about 0.5 cubic centimetres of semen.

This semen needs to be transferred to the hen as soon as possible. Again, two people are required, one to hold the female between the knees and the other to inseminate her by introducing the pipette containing the semen into the oviduct once she is encouraged to be receptive.

The technique of artificial insemination is not difficult but it is much better to learn through an actual demonstration than from the written word. The welfare of the birds should be paramount at all times and it is essential that no damage is done through not understanding any of the correct procedures. There are people in the poultry world willing to provide artificial insemination demonstrations when and if the demand warrants it.

After the hen has laid a clutch of eggs she will go broody and if you want her to incubate the eggs naturally then this is ideal. However, if you don't want her to remain broody this cycle has to be broken, which can be quite difficult. You can put her in a special pen with a wire floor for a few days, along with food and water and as birds do not like sitting on wire it should stop her being broody. If she is 'sitting'

After the hen has laid she will go broody.

in a shed put her outside and if necessary close the door so that she cannot enter until the evening. This is only possible if there is adequate shelter and feed and water elsewhere in the area. She may well sit tight near the door but if offered treats occasionally, it will help to take her mind off being broody. It also helps to place her on a perch with the other turkeys in the evening. Once she begins to perch by herself, you will have broken the broody cycle and if you have done so early enough in the season she may well lay another cycle of eggs again.

The hard work of breeding, in both stags and hens, will be followed by a moulting period. All turkeys moult whether they are wild or domestic. The moult is when the birds lose their old feathers, look really delapidated and grow new ones. This process is a little more complex in the turkey than the chicken because a poult goes through various stages of moult before even becoming an adult. Although poults begin to grow feathers within a week of hatching, many of these will be dropped and replaced as they develop. By the time poults are about 12 weeks old they will have been through three moults but two will only have been partial with some wing feathers retained.

Adult birds have a complete moult in the summer but the timing of this can range from mid-summer through to late autumn. I have even known a hen turkey drop her feathers at the beginning of November and be in a full moult and very bare just as biting cold winds arrived. If you have a similar experience it is worth housing such a bird because they can

The feathers from a moulting turkey have provided ideal nest material for this swallow's nest.

get really chilled and feel quite miserable with no natural covering. Generally it takes longer to drop the feathers than to grow new ones and once the process of growth begins you can almost see the feathers growing daily starting as little stubs with the shafts full of blood, then developing until the birds are once again fully covered in feathers.

This is a natural process but it can help to give moulting birds some supplement in their drinking water. It is quite a stressful period and anything that can be done to assist the birds through this should be considered. During the moult the birds will feel rather self-conscious for they know they do not look and certainly won't feel at their best, so watch for any possible bullying. Also, they will feel physically uncomfortable if handled, especially at the stubbly growth stage, so be aware of this and handle any moulting birds with great care. Once they have the new feathering the birds will look stunning and the big national poultry shows are held during the winter, mainly for the very reason that most birds will be in their best plumage at this time.

Turkeys, like other fowl, can lose their feathers for various reasons such as mites or through fighting. It is as well to know though that they can also drop their feathers if they become immensely stressed or as a last resort in an attempt to escape from a predator (no doubt even more stressed), so NEVER try to catch a turkey by grabbing its feathers. The result will always be just a handful of feathers!

The stag makes his move but is rebuffed.

This hen turkey was receptive and a successful mating took place.

Chapter Seven | The Egg: From Creation to Poult

Raising strong poults begins with the quality of the parent stock. Unless you have fit, healthy birds it is unlikely you will get the hatching results you are after The hen turkeys certainly have their work cut out with regard to egg production. In fact the make-up of the egg is almost as amazing as its creation. The main components are the shell, the shell membranes, the albumen, the yolk, the chalazae and the germinal spot.

The shell, which is mainly calcium carbonate, is quite strong in turkey eggs. It is, however, still porous which allows the oxygen required for respiration to enter the egg and the waste product, carbon dioxide, to escape. Moisture can also be absorbed or escape as required. The inner layer of the egg shell provides the calcium source for the new poult.

There are two shell membranes, both loosely connected. One encloses the whole of the inside of the shell and the other can separate by the air space at the blunt end of the egg. This membrane moves to let the air space increase as the embryo develops and moisture reduces.

The albumen is more commonly known as the 'white' of the egg. This is made up of water, protein, vitamins and minerals and is what the embryo lives on throughout the incubation period. There is a watery outer layer of albumen, then a firm jelly-like central layer and an inner more liquid layer on which the yolk rotates.

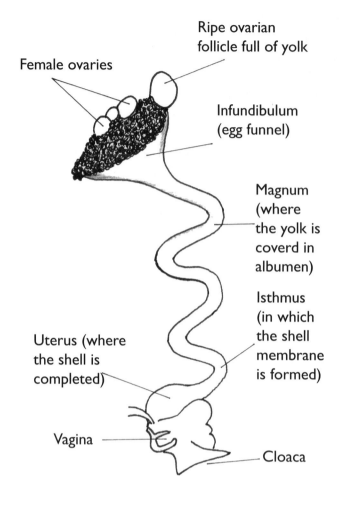

Female ovaries

Ripe ovarian follicle full of yolk

Infundibulum (egg funnel)

Magnum (where the yolk is coverd in albumen)

Isthmus (in which the shell membrane is formed)

Uterus (where the shell is completed)

Vagina

Cloaca

The yolk is collectively water, protein, fats, vitamins and minerals, all contained within a vitelline membrane. It is the 'power house' for the poult as the yolk is absorbed into the abdomen to become the first twenty-four hour feed source when it hatches. The yolk also plays a vital part in the reproduction process because it holds a white spot on its upper surface. This is known as the germinal spot or ova and is the part of the egg where the male and female cells unite to produce a fertile egg.

The chalazae are the two coils of translucent white tissue that are connected from the vitelline membrane to each end of the egg and hold the yolk in the central, rotating position.

To aid the production of premium quality eggs the birds will need a turkey breeder ration that contains the extra calcium and minerals needed. Finding a perfectly formed egg in a nestbox is the end result of a complex cycle which, in a hen turkey, takes place around every 26 hours or so depending on her health, nutrition and environment.

The female ovaries resemble a small bunch of grapes. These are a collection of tiny yolks and each is contained in a delicate membrane follicle. Each yolk contains an unfertilised ovum. As a hen turkey matures and becomes sexually active a yolk will increase in size. When the yolk is ripe the membrane follicle ruptures, allowing it to pass into the infundibulum. The infundibulum is shaped like a funnel and leads into the oviduct passage. The process of the membrane follicle rupture takes place in a specific area designed to allow the yolk to travel down the oviduct without getting in the way of any blood vessels but occasionally the rupture of the membrane follicle causes a blood vessel to rupture as well and this is what causes the blood-spot which you occasionally find in an egg.

Just below the infundibulum the ova are fertilised. This is where the male sperm travels after mating and sperm will remain there and fertilise other ova as they ripen and descend. The yolk then passes down the oviduct into the magnum area where it collects a covering of albumen; then further on, in the isthmus, the shell membranes are formed. Finally, when it reaches the uterus, the shell is secreted. The egg remains in the uterus for a while before moving down to the vagina and being passed out at the cloaca. A turkey egg is generally speckled and this pigmentation is added after the shell has formed. An egg is damp when layed and if you handle it before it fully dries the pigmentation is easily rubbed off. Once dried it is impossible to do this. The drying process provides the egg with a protective 'bloom' which is a natural barrier to mild contamination although it will not prevent any serious contamination.

Once the hens start laying eggs choose only those that are not misshapen and have a good shell with no hairline cracks or ridges, especially at the pointed end. The embryo in eggs that are incorrectly shaped or have other imperfections will not develop correctly and it is not worth taking up space in the incubator with them. Very dirty eggs are also not worth considering as mud or faeces will contain bacteria that could pass through the porous shell and membrane and contaminate the embryo. Even if the shell is washed with tepid water a stain often remains and the damage may already have been done.

The chances of dirty eggs can be lessened by making sure that some type of nestbox or quiet corner is provided in the housing, which encourages the hen turkeys to lay their eggs inside. They are more likely to drop eggs outside where they could get soiled if they are unsure of where they should be laying. If there is little straw or litter in the nestbox an egg can easily be broken and if this happens the birds will take the opportunity of having a good feed. Egg eating is a vice that needs to be stopped as quickly as possible or you could end up with no eggs left for incubation purposes. All traces of a broken egg should be cleaned away as soon as possible. If the birds do start eating the eggs, place some stone eggs or golf balls in the nesting area and collect the real eggs as often as possible.

Careful collection and storage of hatching eggs is another part of successful incubation. Eggs should be collected every day and more than once a day if the weather is hot because the embryo will begin to develop at a temperature above 21ºC (70ºF) but without a constantly maintained temperature it will die. Store the eggs in a Keyes tray (a large egg tray) or on a deep dish of dry sand with the pointed end downwards in a cool, dry room with a temperature of between 10 and 13ºC (50 to 55ºF). The wider, blunt end of the egg contains the air space which should always be kept uppermost. Eggs are most fertile when fresh and fertility will gradually start to decrease after a few days. Ideally, do not store hatching eggs for longer than a week to ten days if you want to have the best chance of success. Whilst the eggs are in storage, rotate them or tilt the tray in opposite directions each day so that the embryo does not stick to a membrane on one side.

If you are going to incubate a large number of eggs then artificial incubation will be the most efficient way of doing so. There is a wide range of incubators on the market but shop around and

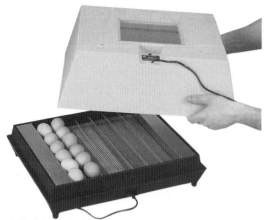

A Polyhatch Incubator.
Photo © Brinsea Products Ltd.

work out what is going to be the most appropriate for you. Cost comes into any decision as well. Prices range from around £60 to £700 and you can pay even more if you want to have a walk in incubator. To begin with the table-top kind, priced at around £200 and which hold about 15 turkey eggs, might well be suitable. The cabinet incubators which look like refrigerators hold a much larger number of eggs and are very easy to use and inspect but expect to pay between £400 and £600 at least. Incubators are also divided up into still air or fan-assisted varieties. The still air ones are usually those that only have one layer of eggs, whereas the cabinet incubator with several shelves of eggs does require fan-assisted air circulation because of the various layers.

When buying an incubator it is better to go for the ones that have moveable egg partitions rather than those with a fixed bar holder. This is because turkey eggs are slightly wider than chicken eggs and unless there is sufficient room for the eggs to roll in between the bars they will need to be turned manually. An automatic turner is also useful because it is sometimes very inconvenient to have to turn the eggs manually. They need to be turned three times a day and the time will always come when you are out and no-one is available to turn them, in which case the eggs sit for longer than they should on one side. Should you feel that you can cope with manual turning, mark the eggs with a cross on one side, it will make it so much easier to see whether the eggs have all been turned or not.

An incubator with an automatic turner is worth its weight in gold as you are not tied to being near it at specific times of the day. With small table-top incubators the turner may be a cradle which the incubator sits on or it could be a tray which moves ever so slowly backwards and forwards.

The incubation period for turkey eggs is 28 days, so from this you can work out how many eggs you want to incubate and this will give you an idea of what to go for. There are numerous poultry and agricultural outlets which sell incubation equipment and poultry magazines and the internet will provide you with lots of contact information as well.

Incubator with turner
Photo © Brinsea Products Ltd.

Once you have your chosen incubator, put it in a room with a constant temperature; only the large cabinet incubators can usually cope with external temperature fluctuations. A back room or spare bedroom would be fine. Do not place the incubator near a door or window where there might be a draught, or where the sun can shine on it at any part of the day. Sunshine on the incubator would dramatically raise the temperature and in doing so would probably kill the embryos. Also, when positioning the incubator, make sure that it is stable and not where it can be knocked off if someone walks by or the dog jumps up. Before switching on the incubator thoroughly read the instructions. This is so very important because the manufacturer will have built it to a specific design which has been tested and therefore the instructions will help you to get the best performance out of that particular piece of equipment. Even though the incubator is new, do wipe it down with disinfectant before use. Good hygiene is a must with any equipment associated with your turkeys.

Double yolked eggs (left) are rare and easy to spot as they are considerably larger than single yolked.

The ideal temperature for the incubation of turkey eggs is 37.5ºC at the centre of the egg. Most incubators will already be set at this but run it for at least 24 hours to determine that it is correct before setting any eggs. Refer to the instruction manual because the reading on the thermometer may need to be a degree higher to be the correct temperature at the centre of the eggs for a particular incubator.

Even though only clean eggs should be used for incubation, they should still be washed in tepid water with egg sanitant added to eliminate any bacteria that may be on the shell. Do not wash them in cold water because this can draw any germs that might be on the egg into the pores and, apart from the fear of bacteria contamination, blocked pores can prevent effective evaporation taking place. The pores of the egg shell have an important role to play during incubation as it is through these pores that the oxygen supply from the incoming air diffuses into the air space and thus into the tissues and blood of the embryo. As the embryo grows, an increase in oxygen is required. In fan-assisted incubators this is already regulated but in the small still air varieties there will be a ventilation hole which can be enlarged for when more air is needed.

It is not only the temperature of the room and incubator that is important but also the humidity level. When it is warm the humidity is higher because warmth produces moisture but when it is

Incubator with turner. Photo © Brinsea Products Ltd.

cold the air is dryer, so the humidity will be lower. Humidity in the incubator is required because without it there would be insufficient moisture in the egg and the membranes would dry up and become hard. In most incubators there are small wells in which to place water to increase the humidity. Again refer to the manufacturer's recommendations. Do not be tempted to over fill with water for if there is too much moisture the embryo will also suffer because not only will there be insufficient oxygen reaching the embryo but it could also drown. This can be a reason for the condition 'dead-in-shell'. The relative humidity in an incubator for turkey eggs should be around 55 %. A wet bulb thermometer will give you the humidity level reading but it can also be determined by the size of the air space in the egg. By candling the egg you can see if the air space is the correct size for the stage of the embryo's development. If it is too small then there is too much humidity and if it is too large then there is insufficient. An alternative way is to weigh the eggs at regular intervals. Throughout the incubation process turkey eggs lose 11 to 13% of their initial weight up to the pipping stage. If this isn't being lost the humidity is too high.

While the incubator is running up to temperature, bring the eggs into the same room so that they can get to room temperature. Then, when they are put into the warm incubator, it will not be so much of a shock. If you have a small incubator, lay the eggs on their side in the tray slots. In larger incubators the eggs can be placed upright, with the pointed end down. Never place an egg blunt end down and pointed end up because the air space is in the blunt end and the chick's head would develop away from the air space causing it to suffocate.

As soon as the eggs are placed in the incubator to begin their incubation the temperature will drop but do not touch the thermostat. The introduction of the cool eggs will lower the temperature but as soon as they warm, the temperature will right itself. Leave the incubator to settle. If the eggs were placed in the incubator in the afternoon and you need to manually turn them, do this before retiring to bed. Then start the routine of turning them three times a day starting the following morning. You must continue to turn the eggs because if you cease to do so nutrients will not make contact with the germinal spot and the embryo could stick to the shell membrane if the position is not changed. To function properly, the internal membrane also needs the egg to turn so that toxic waste products can be extracted.

After the eggs have been incubating for seven days they should be candled to see if the embryo is developing. This can be seen as a blob with blood vessels emanating from it. Should the egg be perfectly clear then it is not fertile and should be removed from the incubator. Although it is possible to make your own candler, there are electric ones on the market and these are reasonably inexpensive and very efficient.

Seeing a hen with her poults is magical

On day 25 of the incubation the pipping process will begin. You may not notice it at the time because the poult will need to peck away at the membrane inside the shell before it actually breaks the shell itself. At this stage, cease the egg turning and increase the humidity a little; this will help the poult to break through the membrane. Do not be tempted to open up the incubator to have a look for it is vitally important that a constant temperature is kept at this point. Possibly, on day 27, and certainly on day 28, there should be activity in the incubator with egg shells breaking all around. Do not open up the incubator but do allow the poults to remain in the environment until their down is fully dry. They will be fine for a few hours. Then move them either to a cosy-brooder, which is a plastic covered area with two bulbs for warmth, or under a specially prepared small area where there is a heat lamp. Transfer another batch of poults when they are fully dried and strong enough to move.

Leave the incubator in case other eggs that have not hatched do so late. However, after two days turn the incubator off as any eggs left are obviously not going to hatch. It may well be beneficial to break open the unhatched eggs to see if there is anything you can learn from them. The poults may be too sticky, in which case the humidity might have been too high, or perhaps they were fully formed but just didn't make it out of the shell in which case the humidity may have been wrong or the temperature may have fluctuated. An essential task then has to be carried out in order to ensure successful hatching in the future. Thoroughly clean and then disinfect the incubator. Electricity and water don't mix very well so don't go sloshing too much water around the operating parts. Bacteria can build up in a warm environment and with dirty shells and defecating poults, sterilising the incubator is absolutely vital.

I hope this does not make artificial incubation sound too daunting. It really isn't that difficult and is actually very straightforward once you get into the routine of what to do but even more importantly, do not be despondent if not all your eggs hatch. It is very rare to have a 100% hatch and as you incubate more you will learn how to gauge all the intricacies and requirements and sometimes you will do brilliantly but there will be other times you may just want to forget. You certainly wouldn't be alone in experiencing either extreme.

As well as artificially incubating some eggs you may want to incubate some naturally as well. A large breed of chicken would be needed for some turkey eggs. A Rhode Island Red or Wyandotte would probably be fine.

Turkeys do make wonderful mothers though and if you have a broody turkey then why not let her have a slice of natural life? It is very important, however, to put her in a quiet place where she will not be interrupted by any other birds and she will be safe. Do remember the earlier warning about the dangers of letting your hen 'sit' under a hedge. You can certainly make up a nesting place which is in a contained area and move her with her eggs and usually she will take to the change with no problem. If she is very broody her eggs will be the most important thing and as long as they remain with her she will be content. You could make up a special broody box but I tend to use a large cardboard box on its side with the flaps just pulled too in the front. Cut some ventilation holes in the side and put some straw or shavings on the floor and inside this darkened box she will be quite content. The beauty of such a broody 'coop' is that you can just burn it once it has served its purpose. A good sized dog kennel is equally good. A secure wired front can be made for it which can be partly covered overnight so that investigating vermin do not frighten her. You will then have a turkey broody coop for outside as well. Should she be the hen of only a pair, then the stag may fret if she suddenly disappears so if she is in a dog kennel with a wire front he will at least be able to see her and will know that she is still about and be quite content but unable to interfere with her.

A broody will need to be taken off the clutch of eggs once a day at the same time each day. I usually do the broody rounds at around 2.00pm and by that time they are ready for a drink, some wheat and then to empty themselves. Wheat will be quite sufficient because she isn't using a great deal of energy whilst brooding and any pellet feed will result in defecating more and possibly dirtying the eggs. The last thing you want is faeces on hatching eggs because bacteria could easily be absorbed through the porous shell. Eating wheat and keeping to a strict routine she will be able to go the 24 hours and empty herself thoroughly when she gets off the nest. Defecating is incredibly important for the welfare of the bird so do not let her go back onto the eggs until she has performed this act. If you carry out the routine at a regular time each day the turkey will get to know the procedure but don't expect her to do it herself as she won't want to leave the eggs!

By day 27 just offer her a drink and a little feed by her side because the eggs may have started pipping and she shouldn't be disturbed. If eggs are pipping and the warm feathers disappear you could lose the poults. Any disturbance and she might accidentally squash the poults with her large legs and feet. Anticipation will keep her going and with drink offered she will come to no harm. If it is possible to check whether she has defecated and just clean it that will be good but if it is likely to worry her then leave it. Often a turkey will move slightly from the area she has dirtied in an attempt to keep the eggs clean.

Hopefully, the next day, hatching will begin and the hen will be delighted with what is going on under her. Offer her a drink but do not leave anything that poults could fall into and drown. A chick drinker and chick feeder with turkey starter crumbs can be placed nearby and she will feed with the poults, probably beginning the following day. I always cook and chop up some hard boiled egg to put in with

If you have a broody hen why not let her have a slice of the natural life and rear some poults?

the crumbs and the poults love this, as does the hen. Do not feed her adult feed because she will call the poults and they would choke on the large pieces.

The turkey hen will probably sit tight for another two days and after that she will have decided that any eggs not yet hatched are not going to and her priority will be with the youngsters. At this point she will get up and just walk around a little. Take this opportunity to remove all the shells, dud eggs and any dirt in the nest area. Put a little fresh litter down so she can brood her poults in a clean bed. Make sure that she is confined in an area with the poults so that she cannot begin to wander around just anywhere with them. This is the natural instinct for wild turkeys but the poults would soon get either lost, killed or would die from damp grass etc. Once she has her poults, leave her to bond and care for her young without too much disturbance. After a few days she will be getting into the routine of you checking the feed, water and bedding and have every confidence in you checking any of the poults, if this is necessary. Most turkey hens take motherhood in their stride but just occasionally there will be one who will be rather overly protective and worry if people are around her.

Hatching your own poults is very exciting whichever way you do it but seeing a turkey hen with her poults is magical and well worth the effort.

Day-olds may not eat on the first day as they will still be absorbing the egg yolk into their system, however, after that they should be encouraged to do so. If they are under a broody turkey or a chicken, the broody will be helping. From day one put some feed onto a plastic tray or chick feeder and place it fairly close to the broody

Chapter Eight | The Young Ones

Poults from an incubator can go directly into the shed in which they will be reared so long as electricity is available. From day-olds to about six weeks they will need some form of heating, especially at night. If there are only a few poults then a cosy-brooder is certainly useful. This is a plastic cover with two electric bulbs in the top which provide sufficient heat to keep the youngsters content. There is an opening at the front and the poults can go in and out as they wish. A cosy-brooder is, however, only suitable for about a fortnight, after which time the poults will need more space and should progress to a suspended heat-lamp. The day-olds could go straight under a heat lamp without using a cosy-brooder; it really does depend on your own personal management preference.

The height of the lamp should be adjusted so that the poults have sufficient heat beneath it to be comfortable. The lamp should be switched on for a while before the poults are in place so that the area can warm up. To begin with, put your hand on the shavings under the lamp where the poults will be sleeping and see how it feels. The poults themselves will also be a guide because they will soon let you know if the temperature is wrong. If they huddle together under the lamp then it is too high and the poults are cold. Sometimes you will even see poults standing under a lamp and so tired that they are swaying but because their sole instinct is to get closer to the heat they just will not lie down. If the lamp is too low and it's too hot underneath the poults will get close enough to feel the heat but will also keep a distance. Therefore, they are more likely to be in a circle just beyond the immediate heat. Contended poults will be evenly spread under the heat lamp, each sleeping under the necessary gentle warmth required.

A lamp is essential to provide a constant heat source.

For the first week or two the poults will need to be in a small enclosure in the accommodation area so that they cannot stray away from either the warmth, the feed or the water. The space they are allocated should be sufficient for exercise, plus room for drinkers and feeders, with ample space under the actual heat-lamp for sleeping. This area can be contained by providing a temporary barrier made of cardboard, plywood or any other suitable material but do make sure that it is stable and cannot fall and squash any poult beneath it. Also, if it is made of flammable material make sure that it is sufficiently far away from the heat lamp not to be a fire risk. A contained area will also prevent draughts affecting the poults which is very important as they can so easily become chilled at this early stage of life.

Make sure that each poult knows how to eat and drink. Turkeys are sometimes a little slow at doing this. As you place each poult in the brooding area, dip the beak into water in the drinker and usually it will sup and when the head is lifted they will swallow. Once they have done that they will be fine and will then drink quite readily themselves. It is vital that poults do learn to drink quickly because they can soon suffer gut problems if they are starved of water.

A few poults will begin to explore their surroundings and start pecking at things even when just a day-old. To encourage eating chop up some hard boiled egg and mix this in with the turkey starter crumbs, then stand back and watch the rush! Poults will usually copy each other so as long as some are eating this will get the others doing so but do gently take a poult and dip its beak into the crumbs if it looks as though it needs encouragement.

Once poults begin to eat with relish they will also begin to defecate constantly. As they run around the area in which they are housed, waste material can accumulate on their toes and feet. If this is not cleaned off regularly it will eventually become a dry, hard ball on the toe or toes, at which point it must be removed but with great care. Never just pull this away as the claw is likely to come away as well. Just pick away, gently, removing the rubbish a little at a time until what is left simply falls away without damaging the claw itself. Adult turkeys can be affected in this way too if not kept on clean litter. To prevent this happening clean the litter on a regular basis. This also prevents any build up of bacteria which, in warm and certainly in damp conditions, can reproduce rapidly.

Occasionally you will get a poult at about three to four days old that will keep falling over. When this happens it is very much like

Make sure the poults know how to use the drinker.

a sheep which is unable to right itself without help. I do not know what causes this but I suspect that it could be something to do with nutrition. Young turkeys grow very quickly and if they are not taking in sufficient sustenance to keep up with this rapid growth they will become weak. I have found that this is soon overcome if you isolate the poult and make sure it feeds very regularly throughout the day. It may even be necessary to put tiny pieces of egg and crumb into the beak and, once it has swallowed, dip its beak in water. Placing it in a small box in the kitchen or wherever you are working is the easiest way of doing this and with this extra attention the poult should become much stronger after only a few days. It can then be returned to the others.

Some poults may get dirty vents or 'sticky bum' as it is often referred to and it should have these faeces removed as gently as possible. Pick away small portions of the faeces while at the same time supporting the rear of the body. Tug away and you could do a lot of damage, especially if any dirt is attached to the inside of the vent. It is important to deal with the problem because, if ignored, the condition will worsen and could totally block the vent area. With no ability to defecate and clear itself the poult would eventually die. A very dirty bottom can be a sign of being chilled or having been in a draught, something to be avoided if poults are not to be disadvantaged during this early part of their development.

As the poults grow, extend the area they use until they are large enough to use the whole shed. If you have alternative accommodation more suitable for growing poults, transfer them when they are off the heat. Depending on the weather and temperature this is usually at around six to seven weeks of age.

Once the poults start to develop, one of the first things that keepers want to know about them is how to tell the sexes apart? It is possible to sex day-old turkeys by looking at the sex organs but this is a skill and damage can be done to the poult if you are unsure of the procedure. This is not recommended unless you have been trained by a skilled person. The sexes can begin to be distinguished by around seven weeks onwards by assessing the physical differences in the poults - although a male can have his wing feathers standing out, a little like an ostrich at only a few days. A male has a slightly larger and longer head, longer back, thicker hocks and larger legs and feet. A female will be daintier, with a head just a little smaller than the male, slightly slimmer legs and smaller feet and toes. When adult the male will have far more fleshy caruncles on his head and neck, whereas the female has a smooth head with some hairs down the back of the head and only a few small caruncles on her neck. She is usually a smaller bird than the male and only the male turkey gobbles.

At about five weeks on warm and sunny days the poults are usually large enough to go outside during the day at which point fencing will be required for a pen. A temporary wired area is suitable for poults until they are larger. This can be made with thin metal stakes threaded through small mesh wire netting and secured into the ground. Fruit cage netting over the top will not only stop poults from trying to fly out but will also prevent any birds of prey from diving onto the youngsters. They will need some shade to protect them from the sun as well. Be aware of the weather and if it turns cooler or looks like rain then return the poults to their housing. It is always better to err on the side of caution, especially in the first few months.

A broody turkey that has been kept housed will be able to take her poults outside at an earlier age because she will brood them whenever necessary. Only let her out in fine weather though or the poults will spend most of the day under the hen. They will also require a protected area so they are safe and relatively confined. Tiny poults could easily get lost if they start wandering around with their mother and they would certainly get chilled if she took them through long damp grass.

If the broody incubated her poults in a turkey coop or dog kennel then a pen can be attached to this and both hen and poults can go in and out as they wish but do continue to secure them in the housing overnight to prevent predators from taking them. The poults can be taken away from the broody at around six to eight weeks. Although she would continue to 'look after them' after that age they will be ready to be treated the same as poults reared artificially. They will also be quite large by then and looking to perch, although some would still choose to cuddle up to the broody if given the chance.

Move poults to more permanent quarters when the weather is kind and the nights are not chilly. You do not want poults huddling up at night for warmth and crowding each other because this could lead to suffocation. If turkeys are comfortable they will not do this. Turkeys can, however, crowd if they are frightened and the greater the number in a house the more serious this could be. Usually, if turkeys have been reared with plenty of contact with humans and things going on around them, they will become more placid and less likely to panic. However, bonfire night for example, with fireworks going off, can be a great worry. To ease this situation, put a mesh covering over any windows so that the turkeys, even though they could obviously hear the noise, are not able to see the fireworks exploding which in itself would be scary. Check the turkeys throughout the evening to make sure they haven't crowded or hurt themselves. They will be used to you going in to see them and if you talk to them so they recognise your voice they should not be frightened by thinking you are a strange intruder. Be careful with a torch because turkeys do not like bright lights shining on them. If this is needed, keep the beam low and away from eye contact with the birds if possible.

On moonlit evenings the turkeys may become very aware of any movement they can see outside and a barn owl flying past would most likely result in a gobble of anxiety.

Some of my turkeys are housed in a large barn and they have the radio on during the day. Even though they can go outside if they wish, it is surprising how they like to stay in, especially when the weather is not too good. In my experience the voices and music from the radio gets them used to background noises and, although it might be difficult to prove, I am convinced that they actually enjoy it.. They will also react to it by gobbling at certain sounds. When the radio is switched off they even seem to know that it is time for bed.

Adult turkeys have wonderful hearing and fantastic eyesight, so prepare to be surprised. Late one evening I could hear gobbling coming from the turkey houses. Usually, turkeys are quiet at night, especially if it is really dark. Concerned, I went to the bedroom window to see if there was anything noticeable. When I opened the window I could hear a car alarm going off in the next village and it was this to which the turkeys were reacting.

Four month old turkeys master the art of keeping alert whilst feeding.

A turkey's eyesight, instinct and alertness is also very acute. When you see a turkey with its head slightly at a slant and glancing into the sky it is probably because it thinks it has seen a predator. What they have seen is perhaps a minute jet aeroplane thousands of feet up. Should a broody hen notice anything like this she will immediately alert her poults and warn them to take cover. These birds are amazing and you can learn so much about their instinct for survival by simply observing them closely over a period of time.

Given the correct feed for their development, daily fresh water, some vegetation and exercise, the turkeys will grow incredibly quickly. Check for parasites every few weeks, worm them regularly and watch for any alteration in behaviour. With this routine you will keep on top of any problems that may occur and the turkeys should flourish.

There is, however, one further thing which you should bear in mind. It is perhaps all too easy to overlook but it is sensible to be more security conscious as it nears Christmas, especially if you are rearing a flock of meat birds. Two legged predators can be just as heartbreaking as a four legged one and a free Christmas dinner could present quite an attractive prospect to thieves. Some locations may be more vulnerable than others but do ask the local police for advice. Make sure that all gates and turkey shed doors are locked. Security lights do help to deter burglars but a big loud dog in the yard is as good a deterrent as anything. Check with your insurer that the turkeys are covered just in case they are stolen. Also, beware what you say to strangers over the phone. If someone is enquiring about what you keep, do be guarded as they might not be a buyer for a butcher but merely trying to weigh up whether it is worth doing a raid! Join a Farm Watch or Neighbourhood Watch scheme and ask neighbours if they would kindly keep a look out for anyone acting suspiciously, in particular in the run up to Christmas.

Chapter Nine | Injuries, Ailments and Parasites

You could be forgiven for reading a chapter with this title and thinking that keeping turkeys is really difficult and perhaps not for you. Yes, some of the diseases are unpleasant and some could result in fatalities. Very few turkeys will, however, experience the problems described here and, if they are looked after in a correct manner, they will most certainly live a long and healthy life without being afflicted by any of them.

However, every responsible turkey keeper should be aware of how their birds can become sick because turkeys can suffer unnecessarily if the owner does not realise there is a problem. The sooner any illness or injury is recognised, the sooner that any possible treatment can be given and the better the chance the bird will have of making a full recovery. Once a bird is ailing it does need to be dealt with immediately as it takes time for any veterinary treatment to begin working and during that time the bird is still losing condition. Therefore, one of the best pieces of advice that can be given is to get to know your turkeys. This may appear to be a rather strange remark but let me put it another way. Time spent in just looking at and being with your birds is never time wasted. You will begin to recognise how they look and behave when they are in the best of health. You will get used to seeing them forage or play in a particular way and will become aware of how much and how often they eat and drink or communicate. Then, when a turkey doesn't react in the way that you are used to seeing, it is usually a sign that something isn't quite right and should be investigated further. This is simply applying good stockmanship and is a valuable skill to develop.

Time spent with your birds is never wasted as you become familiar with their everyday habits and even personalities and can spot if something is wrong quickly.

There are some basics that will be dealt with in other chapters but all birds need to have shelter from inclement weather, nutritious feed, fresh water and a clean, stimulating environment. If you can provide these then you have gone a long way to contributing towards maintaining your turkeys' health. However, just like humans, they do occasionally have things the matter with them that you perhaps had not expected. These can be injuries, a malaise brought on through a change of location, activity, even tiredness, or a bacterial, parasitic or viral infection. Ill health may well be infectious but equally it could be nutritional, a gut or reproductive system disturbance or a dysfunction as in crop impaction, or a prolapse.

The slate stag in the foreground is clearly not well. He is not displaying, he is beginning to droop and he is pale in the head and should be isolatated and checked over immediately.

Aspergillosis

This is a fungal disease caused by *aspergillus fumigatus*. It affects mainly young poults and typical symptoms are gasping for breath, weakness, thirst and drowsiness. The infection causes eye lesions in older birds. A respiratory disease, it is caught through inhaling spores from damp or mouldy litter or feed. Good hygiene is essential to eliminate this problem. Always replace damp litter with dry, dust free quality litter, clean feeders regularly and do not allow stale feed to accumulate in the corners of feeders or feed to spill onto litter which then goes mouldy over time. There is no real cure for this disease. Nystatin, a human medicine that can be accessed via a veterinary surgeon, may be worth considering but is not always effective.

Avian influenza (Fowl plague)

Avian influenza, commonly called bird flu, is a notifiable contagious disease affecting the respiratory, digestive and/or nervous system of any species of bird and causes exceptionally high mortality, especially in turkeys. The cause is a virus, orthomyxovirus type A, and highly pathogenic forms (HPAI) are usually of the H groups 5 and 7. The symptoms of HPAI are quite dramatic, with one of the very first signs being a sudden high death rate. Other signs include a loss of appetite, a drop in egg production, a nasal and ocular discharge, a swollen face, the combs and wattle turning dark blue-black, depression, coughing and paralysis. The low pathogenic (LPAI) form of the disease commonly causes only mild symptoms such as ruffled feathers, a drop in egg production and some respiratory signs but the disease could go completely undetected. Transmission is through direct contact with secretions from infected birds, especially faeces, contaminated feed, water, equipment and clothing. Poults may themselves be affected by broken contaminated eggs in the incubator.

A veterinary surgeon should be called in if there is any suspicion of Avian influenza. Do not take the bird to the veterinary practice in case it is Avian influenza as the risk of spreading the disease must be considered. The vet or the owner then directly notifies the Department for Environment, Food and Rural Affairs (DEFRA) if it looks as though it could be Avian influenza and the Animal Health will be called in to assess the situation and take tests for laboratory analysis.

There is no treatment or preventive at present in the UK as vaccination can only be done with European Commission approval through DEFRA. Any infected birds in an outbreak are culled. To reduce the risk of Avian influenza turkey keepers are advised to keep feed under cover to minimise the attraction to wild birds, keep water fresh and free of droppings, keep waterfowl away from turkeys, control vermin, isolate new stock for two to three weeks, isolate turkeys for fourteen days if they have been taken to an exhibition, change clothes and wash boots before and after visiting other breeders and their flocks, or before and after attending a poultry sale, keep fresh disinfectant at the entrance to poultry areas for dipping footwear or have plastic overboots available, disinfect crates before and after use, disinfect vehicles which have been on poultry premises but avoid taking vehicles onto other premises if possible, wash hands before and after handling your turkeys and comply with any import/export regulations/guidelines.

Avian tuberculosis

Avian tuberculosis is a bacterial infection caused by *Mycobacterium avium* and, although rare, is seen in turkeys kept outdoors which have close contact with wild birds. Transmission is through infected faeces, contamination and fomites. The infected bird will lose a great deal of weight, eventually becoming extremely emaciated. It may also become lame and have diarrhoea. Although this is a very serious disease with no effective treatment, it is possible for a single bird only to be affected in a small group. Confirmation of Avian tuberculosis is at post-mortem. A veterinary surgeon might do a post-mortem on a turkey carcass for you which would show yellow nodules on the intestine and other internal organs, even bone marrow if the bird died of Avian tuberculosis. The regional Veterinary Laboratories Agency may also carry out post-mortems on fresh avian carcasses. There would be a fee for any post-mortem undertaken.

Blackhead (Histomonas) see Worms

Breast blisters

Blisters on the keel bone are caused by inflammation and infection with staphylococcus bacteria. This can be brought on through leg problems and the turkeys continually sitting down on wet or soiled litter. Any leg problems should always be addressed but clean, dry litter is equally important. Breast blisters can also be a symptom of mycoplasma synoviae infection.

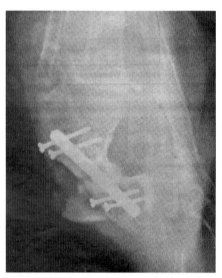

X-ray of Biscuit's pinned leg that made world news.

Broken bones

Turkey bones are quite brittle so landing on hard surfaces from a height without room to glide down gently is never satisfactory. If a turkey breaks a bone it may be possible to mend it under a surgical procedure but this can be expensive and there are very few veterinary surgeons able or willing to carry out such operations. The recuperation process will take many weeks of very careful nursing.

I once had a Bourbon Red stag called Biscuit. He had broken his femur but was operated on at the Queen's Veterinary School Hospital at the University of Cambridge and made a full recovery. Orthopaedic Surgeon Sorrel Langley-Hobbs joined the broken bone with a three inch pin and four screws in an operation that took nearly three hours to complete. It was a first for Sorrel and her team but she believed it was worth a try and it proved to be the right decision because the operation was successful and much was learnt about avian surgery. As this procedure had not been carried out before on a turkey Sorrel wrote a paper about the operation which was published in The Veterinary Record, the British Veterinary Association's journal.

The fact that Biscuit was very used to being handled and his resulting placid temperament certainly contributed to the successful outcome. Had he not been used to such close human contact then the operation may not have taken place at all because it would have been simply too stressful. Of course, such extreme veterinary attention is not an everyday solution but it is quite amazing what can be done for a particular pet.

Broken claws

A broken claw can occur during perching at any age if the bird catches itself awkwardly when turning or descending. This can produce quite a lot of blood and the sight can be quite frightening if red splashes are seen on perches, walls, litter etc., before you have established exactly what the cause is. Never ignore an open wound however small because, even though the environment may appear relatively clean, there will be bacteria lurking and the last thing you want is an infection getting into the wound. With no prevention this can happen in a matter of days with the toe and foot swelling and becoming increasingly painful. The bird then begins to limp because it feels uncomfortable and this then puts it at risk of being bullied by other members of the flock. As soon as you find a bird with a broken claw which has completely detached itself, spray the area with an antibiotic. Terramycin is good for this purpose as it gets into every crevice. Should the claw still be partly hanging, clip it off if it can be done without injuring the bird further and treat it. If the toe has already begun to swell or is only partly severed, then a visit to the vet is the best option. If such a wound is left unattended infection can do a great deal of damage and a veterinary surgeon may have no choice but to amputate the toe.

Bumblefoot

Bumblefoot is a problem which can often occur through descending from too high a perch onto a hard surface causing bruising of the pad, or through a chronic wound that fails to heal. As the injury worsens the lesion enlarges until the foot is greatly distended, particularly the underneath, which is usually ulcerated. This swelling is caused by *Staphylococci* bacteria entering the lesion. It is difficult to treat but antibiotic use will help prevent any further infection developing in the bird and may ease the condition. In extreme cases the ulcerated part breaks away and it is possible to remove a thickened core from the pad. This should immediately be cleansed with antibiotic spray to prevent any further infection from entering. Recovery from bumblefoot does take a long time but, if the suspected cause of the injury is removed and the bird is kept on soft, clean litter, it may well overcome the problem.

Bandaged foot after being treated for Bumblefoot

Cannibalism

This is a behavioural problem that can cause slight injury, severe injury or even death, depending on how soon it is noticed. There are different forms manifested through different reasons. At the youngest stage in life it can be seen through self-inflicting wounds in poults, when they peck at their feet. This is unusual but can happen in one poult in a group. Whatever has triggered the predicament, the poult obviously feels an irritation and pecks at the problem, eventually making the area raw and producing blood, which exacerbates the situation, especially when other poults join in. As it is extremely unusual for the complete group to be affected it is difficult to ascertain the cause. Normally it would be overcrowding, excessive light, too high a temperature, poor feed quality or simply boredom. Check that bedding is clean, ventilation good and the environment not too hot. Although they cannot be prescribed as treatments because neither are licensed for use on poultry, I have found that for a poult that is pecking a toe, rubbing some Germolene or Conotrane on the wound helps to anaesthetise the area and heal the wound. After a few days of treatment the condition will disappear. This problem may lead on from feather pecking: see separate heading.

The worst form of cannibalism is when turkeys set upon one of their group and 'mug' it endlessly, to the death if allowed. The pecking usually takes place around the head and neck area until this part of the body is completely raw, covered in blood and damaged skin tissue. The victim should be removed immediately if this type of serious bullying is suspected. If noticed soon enough the bird can be treated with antibiotic powder and isolated and recovery can be complete after about a fortnight. If left too long the bird is best put out of its misery, or in extreme cases may actually die of its injuries. The best thing to do if this occurs is to change the environment of the other birds. A change of house or transferring to accommodation where they can get outside on grass, with a more interesting environment, can solve the problem. If this cannot be done, try to enrich the environment in the house by hanging up some vegetation for them to peck at. Sometimes it helps to hang up objects that shine or move, such as CDs, which will give them something to investigate. Do make sure that any string hung up does not have lose ends and is high enough for them not to try to eat it and choke!

If there is one particular bully in the group it may well be worth considering isolating it or despatching it. However, the problem with removing birds from a group is that occasionally the 'second in command' sees the main bully gone and simply takes its place, reinforcing the behaviour. Also, it is an extraordinary fact that a turkey being bullied, if put in a different environment, is quite capable of turning round and bullying others. If isolated but with neighbours through a fence, it will try to fight with the bird on the other side, especially a male in springtime. It is possible to reintroduce a bird without any adverse effect but do be prepared for some bullying.

Coccidiosis

Coccidiosis is caused by a small gut parasite, *Eimeria*, which can affect poults from two to sixteen weeks of age but is more often seen in those at three to six weeks. There are seven species of *Eimeria* which infect turkeys but only two tend to cause disease; *Eimeria meleagrimitis* which affects the upper small intestine and *Eimeria adenoides* affecting the caecae and rectum. Symptoms are drooping wings, ruffled feathers, listless, depressed appearance and watery diarrhoea which can be blood stained or have lumps of blood or mucus in it. Toltrazuril, Sulphonamides or Amprolium are veterinary treatments which can be used. As yet there is no specific Coccidiosis vaccine for turkeys in the UK and the chicken vaccine doesn't work on turkeys. Good hygiene is immensely important. The housing and especially the flooring should be cleansed and disinfected thoroughly before poults are placed there. Any damp litter, particularly around drinkers, should be replaced immediately with dry. Biosecurity is also important because of the possibility of transferring Coccidia oocysts from infected faeces via footwear. A coccidiostat (preventive medicine) may be available in proprietary feed but do beware; do not be tempted to feed medicated chicken feed to turkeys as some chicken medications are toxic for turkeys.

Crop impaction

This can happen through the eating of very long grass which doesn't pass through the crop properly and begins to bind up the contents. Although there are solutions which can be tried at home it is better to consult a veterinary surgeon who may have to surgically remove the mass. Birds do recover but the possibility of it happening again should be remembered and consideration given to where the bird is allowed to graze. The condition can also suggest a blockage further down the intestine leading to stasis, e.g. gizzard impaction or MOGPID; mass of grass protruding into the duodenum. This is more likely to occur in spring when there is long lush grass which impacts and could also lead to fermentation in the crop. In a separate condition the crop can become pendulous, whereby it hangs below the normal breastline. Although the cause may be similar to crop impaction, here the muscles are so weak that they are unable to process the food. If this arises consult a vet.

Curled toe

Occasionally a poult can have a curled toe at hatching. This can be as a result of a genetic defect or a temperature fluctuation during artificial incubation. The condition can also suggest a mineral or vitamin deficiency in their mother failing to pass on sufficient into the egg. Although very fiddly, this can be addressed with a tiny splint made of a slither of matchstick and some tape. Medical tape which allows the skin to breathe is better than other kinds but you only need a very small piece and ideally it should be replaced every two or three days to allow for growth. This minute splint will help to straighten the toe during its early development and, after a fortnight or so, it can be removed by which time the toe has usually corrected itself. Such splints however must be light and constantly checked for chafing.

Egg peritonitis

During the egg laying season a turkey could possibly suffer from egg peritonitis. This is when something goes wrong with the egg tube or the egg inside the bird, which consequently cannot be laid. The yolk may miss the funnel of the infundibulum, or the shell may be misshapen and become stuck. The egg may break, introducing infection into the body or it will simply sit in the cavity, eventually becoming toxic. In either case peritonitis will kill the bird. It is possible to diagnose this problem, especially if the hen turkey is in a laying cycle but has suddenly stopped. She will be showing signs of great discomfort and possibly opening and closing her beak as though panting very slowly. This is a symptom of being in great pain. If you handle the bird very gently without putting any pressure on her sides and feel her underneath, this may be distended and extremely hard, just like the top of a drum. At this stage infection is rife and the turkey should be put out of her misery as there is nothing that can be done for peritonitis. This ailment is more common in spring when birds come into sexual activity at the start of the laying season.

Egg bound

This is when a turkey cannot pass the egg comfortably and is similar to constipation. She will stand hunched up and possibly straining at the same time. This is a type of cramp and can be a result of a lack of calcium in the diet or stress. The turkey should be isolated in a warm place and if possible put a little warm olive oil in the vent. If the egg is partially showing then a veterinary surgeon should be consulted.

Turkey with suspected Erysipelas

Erysipelas

Erysipelothrix insidiosa can occasionally be seen in poults and adult turkeys. Among the signs are sudden death or the bird may have a swollen snood, a chronic scabby skin, lameness and depression. Poults have swollen joints. The bacterium can enter through scratches in the skin where stags have been fighting and hence it is seen in stags more than in hens. It can live in the soil for many years and there is an increased risk of it occurring in turkeys if they are kept on land previously used for pigs or sheep. The condition can be treated with antibiotics and a good hygienic environment should keep it at bay. One of the essential aspects of a clean environment is good vermin control. Rats and mice can induce and spread disease so an eradication programme should be put in place to dispose of them.

Favus

These are small whitish growths found on the head and neck and are caused by the fungus *Trichophyton gallinae*. This problem is quite rare and is usually associated with unhygienic living conditions such as stale, dirty litter and unclean feeders and drinkers. It can be treated by mixing formalin in petroleum jelly and, using a rubber glove, gently rubbing the ointment onto the skin.

Feather pecking

Feather pecking is a vice usually seen in birds confined in too small an area or in an environment that offers too little stimulation. Turkeys do like to have interest in their day and if boredom overcomes them they will make their own interest and what they come up with may not be very pleasant. Feather pecking around the neck and vent area is most common. This can begin through birds cleaning their beaks on another turkey's feathers or through boredom, but often the birds will eat the feathers, suggesting that their diet may have something to do with it, for feathers are a form of protein. This behavioural pattern can range from just a few feathers going missing around the neck or tail to complete feathers being destroyed and severe injury on the back of the bird, with the base of the back becoming devoid of any feathers and blood being drawn. Enrich the birds' environment because if not addressed this could lead to cannibalism. Check over the birds for mites because it could be that irritation is causing them to peck at the feathers themselves, which then encourages others to do the same. Provide a good dust bathing area although you will notice that if internal accommodation is cleaned regularly the birds just love dustbathing in fresh shavings. In the summer they will tend to find a good dry piece of soil outside and this will become their dust bath.

Fighting

As winter turns to spring males can become quite feisty with one another. This is perfectly normal and it is the natural process for determining that their genes will be carried forward into the next generation. Even if a group of males have grown up together and have no females around, they will still go through the basic seasonal routine of 'hormones out of control' which usually involves being beastly to their best friends! Stag fights can cause injury but for most of the time these pass without too much of a problem. They will scar each other on the head and eventually one will take a back seat and allow the other to be 'master,' but any serious fighting and damage should immediately be dealt with and the victim removed.

If the scratches are really bad it can allow bacteria to enter wounds so treatment with an antibiotic powder or spray is certainly wise. Full thickness skin tears can lead to large gaping wounds which may need veterinary attention and stitching together. Occasionally, hen turkeys will also fight and this can be quite dramatic for a few days but again, just keep an eye on the situation and they will usually settle down after a while and become the best of pals again. Once separated, especially for more than one or two days, be prepared for fights and bullying on reintroduction. This is why care has to be taken and it is best to reintroduce a bird at dusk when they can then sleep together under the same roof before venturing out together in daylight. If trying to introduce birds that haven't previously lived together it is worth putting them all into a new environment so that they all have something unaccustomed to get used to.

Fowl cholera

This is a highly infectious disease caused by the bacterium *Pasteurella multocida*. It can range from acute septicaemia to chronic and localised infections, along with swollen joints, lameness, coughing and ruffled feathers but is usually first noticed by sudden death. The infection can be present in rodents so it is essential that effective pest control is undertaken. Sulphonamides, tetracyclines, erythromycin, streptomycin and penicillin can be used in treatment but the disease can reoccur so treatment can take a long time to be effective.

Haemorrhagic enteritis

This is a viral disease which results in heavy bleeding in the intestine. The turkeys go off their feed and water and have diarrhoea. Just prior to death bleeding can be seen from the vent. Causes of the disease can be unsuitable feed, contaminated water, a sudden change of environment or poor husbandry. Turkeys can become affected if outside in inclement weather with little or no protection. Treat it with oral tetracyline and the bird will need isolating in a warm, clean and peaceful environment for up to four weeks. There is no effective 'treatment' as this is a viral disease but TLC may facilitate recovery. It is often first seen as a result of a sudden death but closed groups can often build up an immunity to this disease so it may just affect a recently introduced stressed bird.

Hexamitiasis

Hexamita meleagridis is a protozoan parasite transmitted by faeces, fomites and carriers. The bird loses its appetite, then weight and passes a watery diarrhoea before becoming very depressed, eventually going into a coma. Convulsions may take place before death. Tetracycline is used to treat this disease and the bird should be kept in a warm, comfortable environment. If antibiotics are given this is to control any secondary bacteria that may be present. Good hygiene helps to reduce the risk of hexamitiasis, especially regular changing of drinking water and thorough scrubbing of drinkers or troughs. It may be a problem in birds drinking from dirty puddles, so avoid poached areas in pens. The disease can also evolve when groups of turkeys of differing ages are mixed.

Leg problems

Turkeys can suffer from various conditions which will affect their legs. Perosis is one such condition that can easily be avoided with good nutrition. Perosis is a thickening, shortening and distortion of the bones associated with a deficiency of calcium, phosphorus, manganese and choline in the ration. If turkey poults and growers are given an appropriate proprietary ration for their age this disease should not occur.

Perosis should not be confused with a condition of newly hatched poults called 'spraddle legs.' This is likely to be linked to a fault during incubation or improper diet of the parent stock. In turkeys the metatarsus often turns at a right angle so the legs are actually splayed. There is no actual cure for this problem but it may be possible to make a small support in the form of a tiny figure of eight tie which draws the hocks together and can, over the course of a week or two, remedy the problem. Then, with correct nutrition, the poult can recover. Any such support will need to be changed after a few days to allow for growth and to prevent any restriction.

Adult turkeys could also suffer from a slipped tendon. It is, in fact, vitally important not to catch turkeys by a single leg because joints can so easily slip out. The worst scenario is that the lameness is caused by a tumour but the condition of the rest of the bird could well give a clue as to whether this is the problem or not.

There are a number of infections occurring in turkeys that affect legs, so it is not always easy to immediately determine the problem unless other factors are taken into account or dismissed accordingly. Mycoplasmas can swell the leg joints causing lameness; Ornithobacterium infection (ORT), which has similar symptoms to Mycoplasma, can affect the use of the legs or turkeys can simply sprain or even just bruise themselves which can cause lameness for a while. If, after inspection, disease can be ruled out then the pain of a sprain or bruising can be eased for a while by giving the turkey a basic aspirin tablet.

Very heavy mature turkeys can develop leg problems. If hybridised turkeys in particular are kept as pets this should be taken into consideration and a suitable diet and plenty of exercise given. Occasionally it is just not possible to work out why a turkey is lame and even on veterinary inspection no clear diagnosis can be made. Usually a course of antibiotics will be advised and often, with good care, the birds do recover.

Lice
Lice are insects with flattened bodies that live on the skin or feathers of turkeys. They are more often found around the vent area because this is where they find moisture and lay their eggs. Although poults, once outside on grass, may become susceptible to lice, it is the adult birds and in particular the stags that more readily catch these parasites. Lice are yellowish-brown in colour and can easily be noticed if feathers are parted, especially around the vent, thighs or wings. There are two species of lice that are found specifically on turkeys and three other species that are chicken lice but if turkeys are kept close to or with the chickens, they may catch these as well.

Goniodes meleagridis (Large turkey louse)
The large turkey louse will be the most commonly found and easiest to spot.

Lipeurus gallipavonis (Slender turkey louse)
This louse affects turkeys in the same manner as the large turkey louse but this, as with the *Liperus heterographus* (Chicken head louse) will be seen on close inspection on any part of the turkey, even running around the head of the bird. *Eomenacanthus stramineus* (Chicken body louse) and *Menopon gallianae* (Chicken shaft louse) can also transfer to turkeys.

Fortunately all forms of lice can be controlled quite easily with louse powder but if left untreated they can cause problems. The affected turkeys will gradually lose condition as their health is being challenged and if a stag is heavily infested, especially around the vent area, it may interfere with his ability to mate. If a spot-on parasitical treatment is used it will kill all lice and mites.

Mites

Mites are miniscule eight-legged parasitic insects which can cause great harm and even death if left untreated. Unlike lice, which do not appear to irritate birds greatly, mites will cause considerable irritation, eventually becoming a major welfare problem. Most mites use blood or lymph for food so anaemia is a constant symptom. Apart from the direct detrimental effect on its host, blood-sucking mites could easily transmit bacterial and viral infections.

Cytodites nudus (Air-sac mite). This is a mite which lives as an internal parasite in the bronchi, lungs, air-sacs and bone cavities of birds. It does affect turkeys but is not common. The mites are extremely small white specks and how birds become infected is not known. Heavy invasions have been associated with a rapid loss of weight, whereby the birds look very similar to those affected by avian tuberculosis. As the parasite is internal it is difficult to give an accurate diagnosis without a post-mortem and is difficult to treat. A prevention routine such as that for red mite would be useful.

Dermanyssus gallinae (Red mite). This troublesome mite is more associated with chickens than turkeys but turkeys can be affected if kept together with chickens in infested houses. During the daytime these mites live in crevices within the housing and on perches and then climb onto the birds at night, sucking their blood. The red mite can inflict great damage because the birds can become anaemic and will subsequently lose vitality and condition. Always check perches to make sure that no spots of grey powder are present as these are red mite eggs. If these are identified, cleanse the housing thoroughly with products specifically designed to deal with red mite such as Duramitex or Poultry Shield.

Knemidocoptes mutans (Scaly-leg mite). The scaly-leg mite lives in the skin of the bird, burrowing underneath the scales on the legs and feet and causing them to lift and form crusts. Turkeys are not as susceptible to this mite as are fowl but when it does occur the irritation caused is so intense that the birds begin to continually look under their body at the legs, eventually stamping around and pecking at both legs and feet. Vaseline rubbed well into the affected area will help to suffocate the mites. Benzyl benzoate is a white liquid available from veterinary surgeons that can be wiped into the scales in the same way. Eprinex or Ivomec can be used and both are effective but these treatments are not licensed for poultry. They can be ordered through a vet or a qualified agricultural merchant. It is recommended that you administer no more than seven drops on the skin at the base of the neck for an adult turkey. This treatment will kill all external and many internal parasites. It will take at least a year for the legs and feet to return to normal after treatment. The scales will moult but new ones will grow which will not be distorted if the mites have been killed. Do not attempt to pull off crusty scales as there will be raw flesh underneath and this will be extremely painful for the bird, with no advantage gained.

Knemidocoptes gallinae (Depluming mite). This mite is very similar to the scaly-leg mite and only occasionally infests turkeys. It burrows into the skin beneath the base of the feathers. Treat an infestation with Eprinex drops as for scaly-leg.

Liponyssys sylviarum (Feather mite). This can be found living amongst the feathers on the neck and rear of the bird. Anti-mite sprays containing pyrethrum will quickly help the situation but they can also be treated in the same way as depluming mite.

Mycoplasma gallisepticum (M.G.)

A chronic respiratory disease often accompanied by severe sinusitis. It can be passed on through the egg or through direct contact with infected birds and fomites. Turkeys which recover from this disease can remain infected for life, albeit in a dormant form. If the bird then experiences stress or is inflicted in any other way, mycoplasma can recur. A turkey with mycoplasma looks as though it has a very bad cold, with coughing, nasal and eye discharge, swollen sinuses, possible leg problems and a loss of appetite. Antibiotic treatment will be needed but it may help the bird to very gently massage the side of the face toward the beak. Pus will then exude from the nasal opening. Until treatment begins to work the sinus will fill up again but in the meantime you will have removed at least some of the pressure from the turkey's face which should make it feel a little more comfortable.

Mycoplasma iowae (M.I.)

This is a disease which affects unhatched turkey embryos and leads to poor hatchability, the infected embryos being stunted with likely down or feather abnormalities. Infection has largely been removed from commercial breeding stock in the UK.

Good biosecurity is essential to keep any of the mycoplasma infections out of your flock. Always isolate newly bought birds for a fortnight before mixing them. Treatment will reduce the clinical signs but may not rid the bird of the actual infection. Mycoplasmas are so varied in their susceptibility that the birds may respond more favourably to one antibiotic over another. Tylan, Baytril, Pulmotil AC, Tiamutin, Lincospectin and Aureomycin can each be used. Some are given in the drinking water, others will be injected through the breast muscle.

Mycoplasma meleagridis (M.M.)

This is a disease causing respiratory and skeletal problems in turkeys. It also causes poor growth in growing birds and reduced hatchability in breeders, leg problems, crooked necks, stunting and slow growth. Transmission is venereal with infection passing through the eggs and it can be brought on through stress and other respiratory infections.

Mycoplasma synoviae (M.S.)

This is a mild respiratory infection which can become more severe if combined with some other infection. It can lead to coughing, air sac damage, a loss of condition, leg problems and breast blisters. There are different strains of M.S. causing varying degrees of the disease. Having a blood test taken is the only way you can be sure that the bird has *Mycoplasma synoviae.*

Mycosis

Mycosis is a term for any disease caused by parasitic fungi. If a piece of skin is affected by fungi it is described as being mycotic. Fungi can attack the unfeathered parts of the head of a turkey. This is called Favus. A yeast-like fungus growing in the lining of the crop or the mouth is called Thrush *(Moniliasis)* and a fungal infection in the respiratory tract is called *Aspergillosis* (see also under the separate heading).

Newcastle Disease (Fowl pest)

Newcastle Disease is a notifiable disease caused by the virus paramyxovirus PMV-1. It is highly contagious and the birds exhibit nervous signs and paralysis with loss of appetite, coughing, diarrhoea, depression and a drop in egg production. These symptoms can be associated with other diseases but the difference here is that the birds will suddenly die and the death of a group of birds should always ring alarm bells. A veterinary surgeon can give a general diagnosis but laboratory tests will confirm whether or not the birds have contracted Newcastle Disease. This is potentially a very serious viral infection which means that any suspicions must be reported to the Department for Environment, Food and Rural Affairs (DEFRA) without delay. In the event of an outbreak, all infected birds are culled and movement restrictions are put in force by DEFRA. It is possible to vaccinate against Newcastle Disease but it is best to consult your veterinary surgeon as to whether the disease risk in your area is sufficient to warrant this.

PEMS

Poult enteritis and mortality syndrome (PEMS) is an infectious and transmissible viral disease capable of causing sudden or lingering death in poults between seven and twenty eight days of age. It causes gut ache, feed refusal with birds flicking feed out of feeders and can lead to severe stunting and poor growth. Affected poults show hyperactivity and are more vocal than usual. They drink lots but eat little, becoming increasingly weak. The droppings are a watery pale brown and the birds huddle up together trying to keep warm. A range of antibiotics are useful but flouroquinolone antimicrobials can also be effective. A good quality poult diet is essential and multivitamins and milk replacers add to the nutritional support. Good hygiene and biosecurity are so important in helping to keep diseases such as PEMS at bay.

Poult injuries

Growing poults can be quite mischievous and like to jump and fly onto any object they can. Damage can be done during this exploratory phase and it has been known for them to break their necks whilst descending from a height – even a straw bale. It is therefore important not to have anything which can encourage this type of behaviour before they are more fully developed. The natural instinct of getting high to perch overnight is certainly inbuilt and even poults of just a fortnight old sometimes try to perch. During the first three months of life a turkey's bones are relatively soft and still developing so it is best not to allow them to perch, especially on narrow poles, until after this time. This will prevent any denting in the breast bone which could, in later life, make a table bird look less presentable and disqualify an exhibition bird. Bales of straw to jump on are, however, quite acceptable once the poults are at least six or seven weeks old.

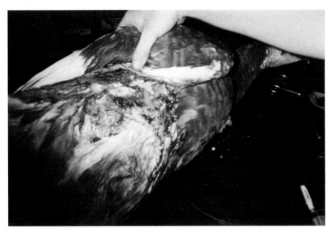

Ripped back and side caused by an over zealous stag 'treading' during mating.

Ripped back

Sometimes hen turkeys are injured during mating. This can be quite traumatic and the injuries may need veterinary attention. Stitches may be required and antibiotics given to stem any infection if the rips are deep. Otherwise scratches can be dealt with by antiseptic powder or spray. Isolate the injured hen from other birds. Saddles should be used on hens that are mating naturally. See Chapter Six, Doing What comes Naturally.

Salmonella infections

The term salmonella represents a huge group of bacteria, probably more than 2,000 different types, which can infect a large number of animal species including humans. Fortunately, only a few are likely to infect poultry and even fewer are associated with disease in turkeys. In most cases the salmonella just sits in the birds intestines and causes no problems. However, certain types have the capacity to cause disease, especially if your bird is already ailing for some other reason. Salmonella is likely only to really be a problem for young poults.

Although antibiotics may help once a turkey is infected the approach must always be to reduce the likelihood of infection in the first place. This can be achieved by following the highest standards of hygiene with your birds but especially by controlling any contact with rats, mice or wild birds. Incidents of salmonella infection associated with certain more significant types have dramatically decreased in recent years following vaccination of commercial flocks.

Salmonella pullorum (BWD bacillary white diarrhoea)

Although all ages of turkeys can be affected by salmonella pullorum, it is the very young poults that it can rapidly kill. It is transmitted from affected breeders through the egg. However, it can pass horizontally in young birds and is sometimes associated with cannibalism. The turkeys suffer from a white diarrhoea, depression, ruffled feathers and closed eyes. They cheep loudly, gasp for air and are sometimes lame. Amoxycillin, tetracyclines and flouroquinolones are used as treatment. Although the bacterium can survive for many months it is susceptible to appropriate disinfectants.

Salmonella paratyphoid

This salmonella bacteria is capable of causing *Enteritis* and *Septicaemia* in young poults. Transmission may be through shell contamination but once established it can remain in the local environment and in any rodent population. The infection is spread by faeces, fomites and poorly stored contaminated feed. Birds more readily succumb to the disease if they are not on a balanced diet, have been chilled, do not have an adequate fresh water supply or already have a bacterial infection. They will have ruffled feathers, closed eyes, diarrhoea, vent pasting, will lose their appetite and will look thoroughly dejected. Treatment is through Tetracycline, Amoxycillin or Fluoroquinolones. Thoroughly disinfect housing, feeders and drinkers, etc. and make certain that feed is stored in a clean, dry and wild bird and rodent free area.

Salmonella typhimurium and Enteritidis

These are the Salmonella bacteria often associated with human food poisoning so it is important to always consider personal hygiene and wash hands thoroughly after cleaning out or handling birds. Salmonella infection is found in poultry worldwide and this includes turkeys. The signs of disease and predisposing factors of disease are similar to those of salmonella paratyphoid. The bacteria generally live in the intestines and can be carried by contact with infected faeces, fomites and contaminated eggshells. Vertical transmission is through infected breeders via contamination of the egg yolk or through eggshell contamination. The bacteria survives successfully in the environment but can be controlled by suitably concentrated disinfectants. Treatment is the same as for salmonella paratyphoid and good hygiene and management is essential in controlling and preventing this disease. This should also include the control of vermin and prevention of any contamination from wild birds.

Thrush *(Monialiasis)*

This disease, which is also called sour crop, is caused by monilia fungi and can be extremely debilitating to the bird as it grows, primarily in the crop, but it can also be found in the mouth and gizzard. It is a yeast and takes the form of tiny cream coloured ulcers that, together, look like a mass of curds and can, over time, completely line the crop. It is one of those diseases that is not obviously noticeable but an affected turkey will become listless and lose its appetite along with loss of weight, especially on the chest. Unfortunately, it is a disease that can only be confirmed on post-mortem but if this is what the bird is suffering from it can be quite dramatic when seen. Thrush is another of the diseases which arise as a result of unhygienic conditions, mainly in equipment. Treatment is difficult because the fungus will 'feed' on antibiotics, so these should not be administered. Nystatin is worth trying.

Transmissible enteritis (Bluecomb)

Bluecomb in turkeys is a viral disease that was first recognised in America in 1944 amongst birds on muddy ranges. It may be coincidental that the pasture was muddy but it is certainly known that mud harbours healthcare problems so these conditions should be avoided if at all possible.

Bluecomb can affect a complete group of turkeys at once and the mortality rate varies from very few to all. Transmission is through infected birds or faeces. The turkeys become anorexic, depressed and their body temperature falls so they huddle together for warmth. The head darkens, crops are sour and they pass loose brownish droppings. It is treated with antibiotics. Both Terramycin or Aureomycin are effective. You must also keep the birds warm and their litter clean.

Tumours

Unfortunately, as in all other animals, turkeys can be affected by tumours, i.e. lumps and bumps. Although there are several diseases that can manifest certain symptoms, if these possibilities can be ruled out with treatments it may come down to the presumption that illness could be caused by a tumour. If a turkey appears to be quite healthy and then exhibits an inability to stand without wobbling, it could well be that a tumour affecting the spinal chord could be the problem. Symptoms will probably depend on where the tumour is located but loss of weight or simply a miserable bird may be the first you know. Sadly this is usually when the tumour has grown quite a bit and damaged organs so the prognosis will inevitably be very poor. A veterinary surgeon will do everything possible to eliminate other illnesses, eventually treating it with steroid injections but if the bird continues to decline it will be in its own interest to put it to sleep.

Turkey coryza

This is a respiratory disease associated with *Bordetella avium*. It causes a loss of voice, eye and nasal discharge, snick (sneezing), failing appetite and difficulty in breathing. Antibiotics do little to treat this disease so a clean environment with good ventilation for the birds is essential. Good drinking water hygiene is necessary and soluble vitamins or poultry tonic in the water will aid recuperation.

Turkey rhinotracheitis (TRT)

A disease of turkeys caused by the pneumovirus genus *Paramyxoviridae*, this can be passed from bird to bird but can also be transmitted by fomites. The turkeys have a failing appetite, loss of voice, swollen sinuses, nasal and eye discharge and swollen heads as typical signs, especially in young birds. Adult birds also produce thin-shelled and depigmented eggs. Antibiotics are not effective so make sure the birds are in a clean, dry and dust-free environment, with fresh multivitamin drinking water. It is possible to vaccinate against TRT but if only a few turkeys are kept and their environment is hygienic it should not be necessary.

Turkey viral hepatitis

An unidentified virus causes this infection in turkeys. It brings about depression and occasional death in birds which appear to be in an otherwise good condition. During post-mortem analysis haemorrhaging may be seen. There is no treatment but with good husbandry many birds do recover. Turkey viral hepatitis is another disease that should not manifest itself if the birds are kept in a clean, dry and dust-free environment.

Worms

Just like cats, dogs and other animals turkeys can become infested with worms and they should be treated for such on a routine basis. There are various types that live in different parts of the body.

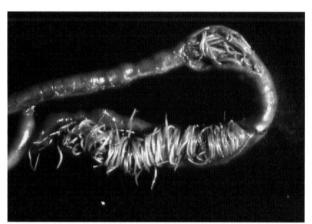

A severe case of roundworm has blocked the intestines causing them to rupture.
Photo © Janssen Animal Health

Ascaridia dissimilis (Roundworm) is the most common and can be a serious threat. Although there may only be a few adult worms in a turkey's intestines, from these will develop numerous larvae, which will have a significant affect on the bird's health. Birds may just be unthrifty or may lay smaller eggs. Roundworms are capable of causing a necrotic-like enteritis and subsequent E.coli infection as well as migrating to other parts, in particular the liver, and causing damage. A severe infestation of roundworms can block the intestines, even causing them to rupture and may be visible in the bird's droppings.

Capillaria contorta (Hairworm) is a thin, hair like pale coloured roundworm which can be anything from 7 to 18mm in length and infests the crop and oesophagus. *Capillaria obsignata* is found in the small intestine. Infection is through the oral route. These worms, although small, can do a lot of damage and can be very debilitating to the affected birds.

Cestodes (Tapeworm) is a segmented parasitic worm which attaches itself to the small intestine by the head. Growth is from the head outwards so the segments furthest from the head are the ripest and contain the eggs. These segments containing the eggs will break away and will eventually be passed out of the turkey's body via the droppings. The minute eggs are then ingested by a smaller being such as an insect, slug or earthworm, whereupon they hatch. The turkey then becomes infected when it eats the insect that contains the tapeworm cyst. There are many different species of tapeworm that turkeys are hosts to and these can vary from miniscule worms to some around 25 cms (10 inches) in length. All too often you won't even know that your birds have tapeworms.

Heterakis gallunarum (Caecal worm) is a nematode parasitic worm up to 1.5cm in length that is found in the caecum. It causes inflammation of the caecum but more importantly it can carry another parasite, *Histomonas meleagridis,* which causes blackhead.

Histomonas (Blackhead) is the disease of most concern to turkey keepers and more often than not it is fatal. *Histomonas meleagridis* is a protozoan parasite which chickens can carry but turkeys, pheasants, game birds and peafowl are the most susceptible. The parasite is ingested in the ova of heterakis worms or as larvae in earthworms and the incubation period is fifteen to twenty days. The main sign of blackhead is a sulphur yellow diarrhoea, depression with head sunken into shoulders, a lack of appetite and emaciation. The parasite attacks the liver which is why the condition is often fatal. It is difficult to cure as the drug which has in the past been successful in dealing with this disease, Dimetridazole, has been banned from use in the European Union. Metronidazole is now used in the form of Flagyl tablets. Another product is Stomorgy 110 which contains Metronidazole plus Spiromycin. Good hygiene and fresh pasture help to prevent blackhead occurring. It is never a good idea to put turkeys on land which has been inhabited by chickens, especially if it has been occupied by them for a long period.

Syngamus trachea (Gapeworm) is a nematode parasitic worm which, as the name suggests, lives in the turkey's windpipe. They can infest this part of the anatomy so severely that the bird chokes, hence the 'gaping' for breath implied by the name. Infection is via the oral route with earthworms, slugs and snails being the hosts but it is also possible for the turkey to ingest the embryonated egg directly. Gapeworm is more likely to affect free range birds, especially where gatherings of wild birds are present, for instance, near a rookery.

Evidence of gapeworm infestation can be clearly seen through the bird gaping in a desperate attempt to breathe and in a heavy infestation of roundworm it may be possible to see worms that have been excreted in the faeces. Any turkey with worms will gradually lose condition, become rather mopey and listless and will begin to lose weight. By the time worms are really affecting the system diarrhoea will also be apparent. It is vital that turkeys are treated for worms because poor condition could eventually lead to death.

Treating for worms should never be done on an only when you remember basis! You will need to have in place a regular programme of deworming with the aim of keeping the birds free of adult, egg laying worms. Flubenvet is licensed by the Veterinary Medicines Directorate (VMD) for worm treatment which is incorporated in the feed. Worming may need to be as frequent as every six weeks, especially if turkeys are with chickens when all the birds need be treated and this way the life-cycle of internal parasites will be interrupted. Flubenvet comes as a powder that is mixed in with the feed and can only be purchased from a veterinary surgeon or a qualified agricultural merchant as it is a Prescription Only Medicine (P.O.M). Dosages are clearly marked on the container for large flocks but for these it is also possible to purchase proprietary feed with the medication already incorporated. For just a small number of turkeys the recommended dosage is one tablespoon to 1.8kgs (4lbs) of feed. In order to dose for tapeworm it is recommended that a veterinary surgeon is consulted as the dosage is higher and will depend on the purpose for which the turkeys are kept. A new product launched in 2006, Solubenol, is a wormer licensed for chickens but is also effective in turkeys. It is soluble and is designed to be administered in the drinking water.

Some of the biggest health challenges to turkeys are via the gut so the aim is to keep this part of the bird as free from bacteria and parasites as possible. The pH level of a turkey's gut is 4, ideal for many of the bugs that will try to invade it. By altering this level and making the gut slightly more acidic it becomes a less hospitable environment, making it more difficult for them to pass through and go on to damage vital organs. I have found that putting just a little cider vinegar in the fresh drinking water each day has shown some benefit so perhaps this is one way of creating a healthier gut.

When worming turkeys all litter should be replaced because there will be immediate reinfestation if litter or faecal material is contaminated with worm eggs. The cleaner you can keep the housing and equipment, the better chance you will have of minimising any build up of worm eggs.

Contrary to what some turkey keepers experience I have found that these birds do actually have a great will to live and if kept as pets they will certainly put their trust in you and can display great bravery. However, every injury or disease should be assessed by the owner and the veterinary surgeon together and each situation dealt with according to its severity, the overall demeanour of the bird and what the owner is prepared to undertake both financially and as a nursing commitment. For complicated surgical treatment the veterinary surgeon would probably refer the patient to a specialist but even for general turkey care there are poultry vets that are willing to provide a general practitioner with a second opinion.

Unfortunately there will be sad occasions when nothing can be done to save a turkey from dying, in which case the bird has to be despatched by a trained person or anaesthetised by a vet. However, if you and your veterinary surgeon have done whatever is possible to treat the problem and relieve the pain you will, as an owner, have done the best for the bird.

The veterinary information and advice given in this publication is given in good faith and no liability in respect of diagnosis or application or treatments is accepted by the author or publisher.

Veterinary medicines are regularly reviewed by the European Union Veterinary Standing Committee and more specifically the Veterinary Medicines Directorate in the UK. In time, medicines suggested in this book may be withdrawn or replaced by others. A product which is used to treat a condition in a species for which it is not authorised (licensed) is only possible if the product is prescribed by a veterinary surgeon who knows the birds involved and in circumstances where no product authorised for the conditions and species being treated is available. In this case veterinary surgeons may, on their own responsibility, prescribe for animals under their care, medicines for a use that is not in accordance with the manufacture's authorised recommendation (off label use).

If your bird is used to being handled it makes operational procedures under local anaesthetic less stressful for the bird, owner and vet!

The vet removes the cyst under local anaesthetic.

A cyst forms on the head of an exhibition bird.

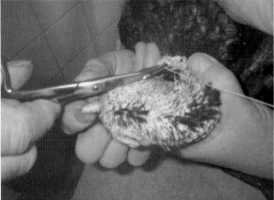

Stitches are applied.

Back home soon after the operation having lunch.

Chapter Ten | Back to the Future?

Organically reared food is definitely increasing in popularity. Fruit, vegetables and meat, both organic and conventionally grown and reared, are transported hundreds of miles from where they are produced to the eventual consumer and the groundswell of wanting to buy locally grown environmentally friendly produce is burgeoning. Consequently there could be a very profitable opening for you if you chose to produce your turkeys according to the principles of the organic farming movement.

However, a considerable amount of homework will be required prior to starting up a flock of organically reared turkeys for the Christmas market. Yes, you would be able to sell them at a premium but there are other things to consider before deciding that this is the route for you. Organic production can be considerably more expensive than conventional and there are some very strict rules to which the participant must adhere.

You cannot just call turkeys organic because they free range on grass. Organic farming is a legally defined form of agriculture, and before any turkeys can be marketed as organic, strict conditions set at UK, European and International level must be fulfilled. A producer also needs to be registered with one of the organic certification bodies, each of which has its own symbol and EU code number.

Any turkey sold as organic must, by law, have a certification symbol and code number linked to

it. The certification symbol or code number tells the consumer that the turkey has met the government's requirements for organic food production. Each certification body within the UK is given a UK code and although you don't need to have the symbol on your produce the code must be shown. The Soil Association is the UK's largest organic certification body and its organic symbol appears on approximately 70% of all organic food produced in the UK. Its code is UK5. This number does not refer to how stringent standards are but the order in which the government department received the application from the certification body.

Most farms describing themselves as organic have undergone a two year conversion period before full organic status is achieved although a progressive conversion is allowed depending on the history of the land, the current status of grass management, what you intend to grow or rear organically and various other factors.

Under an organic system turkeys must have continuous and easy daytime access to pasture which must be well covered with suitable vegetation. During adverse weather conditions they may be temporarily contained in the house but must not be permanently housed. The turkeys should have access to shelter at all times and be protected from predators. Adequate cover, either by trees, shrubs or cover crops and/or artificial screens, must be provided in free range areas. This cover is to provide them with a form of natural habitat and some protection from the wind and sun.

Organic certification schemes cover every area of production and processing to meet high standards of animal welfare and health. Under an organic system growth-promoting drugs are banned and vaccination can only be used if there is a known disease risk on the farm or neighbouring land which cannot be controlled by other means. The routine use of antibiotics is not allowed but a course of antibiotics to treat a specific problem and prevent unnecessary suffering is acceptable.

Organic farmers are encouraged to choose slower growing varieties of turkey, which are well suited to free range systems. The turkeys can be bought in as organic breeding stock or organic poults. However, at present only a limited number of organic poults from organically managed parents are available. If they cannot be sourced you can apply to the certifying body for permission to buy non-organic poults instead. These poults must be bought in at less than three days of age and managed to organic standard for at least 10 weeks. Once organic turkey producers have their own flock they tend to find it easier to breed their own poults and will buy in extra only if they are unable to produce the number required to satisfy their market.

Sourcing organic birds is not the only hurdle to overcome because how you slaughter and process the birds also has to be addressed. There are very few slaughtering and processing facilities in the UK for organic livestock, let alone organic turkeys. Again, it could come down to the organic turkey producer slaughtering and processing on-farm. This may sound quite daunting but think of the advantages; there is no transportation of live turkeys involved so stress levels are kept to a minimum; the birds would be handled in the main by people they are familiar with; you would be in control of where and when they were despatched and processed and you would have an excellent sales and marketing pitch for your area in that your stock would consist solely of local birds and the food miles involved in their production would be almost non-existent.

It must, however, be stressed that to sell organic turkeys you need to identify your market beforehand, your facilities will probably need to be suitable for slaughtering and processing on-farm and the waste has to be disposed of in accordance with waste regulations.

Organic hatching eggs and eating eggs can only be produced from birds kept on land managed to organic standards. If there are no organic turkeys available then non-organic birds can be bought in to lay eggs if they have previously been reared to organic standards with regard to feed and veterinary treatment requirements. They cannot be bought in after they are eighteen weeks old and must be managed to full organic standards for at least six weeks before any eggs can be sold as organic.

As part of the registration process the organic turkey keeper must provide the certification body with a plan which explains how many birds will be needed each year, how many may be expected to come from available organic sources and how many from non-organic. He must also outline in the plan what he is going to do to ensure that he can get organic birds in the future. Organic

Bourbon Reds prove ideally suited to free range production.

certification will not permit the purchasing of birds which have had their beaks either clipped or tipped.

To ensure that organic standards are met and kept, the turkey producer certified is visited annually by an inspector when all the turkey rearing and processing activities are checked. Spot checks are also made and these are carried out unannounced.

Rearing organic turkeys requires commitment and there are both setting up and registration costs involved. Organic feed such as organic wheat is more expensive than its conventionally grown equivalent but some manufacturers produce turkey feed that is suitable for organic as well as conventionally reared birds.

Having given you just a feel of what rearing organic turkeys is about I suggest you talk to a member of the technical staff of one of the organic certifiers about the best way to proceed if you wish to do so. They can discuss agronomic, management and marketing factors which will apply to your situation and location. Producing organic food for consumers is challenging but is also very rewarding and certainly the demand for the product is out there. A complete list of the current UK organic certification bodies is listed in the appendices under useful contacts.

It is certainly very interesting that organic certifiers support the slower growing turkey varieties in organic systems. This can only encourage future keeping and rearing of these older types of turkey and there is now research to endorse the claim that they should be promoted for outdoor rearing and sustainable agriculture.

Research carried out during 2003/2004 in America confirms that the traditional standard turkeys are better suited to free range production than the industrial commercial birds. The American Livestock Breeds Conservancy (ALBC), the Virginia Polytechnic Institute & the State University in Blacksburg (Virginia Tech.) and eight breeders and producers of standard turkeys collaborated to compare standard turkey varieties and an industrial strain for immune functions and performance in free range production systems.

The project began with field trials conducted on eight farms across America. Each raised two flocks of thirty birds; a mixed flock of male and female Bourbon Reds obtained from Privett Hatchery in Portales, New Mexico and males only of medium sized industrial Broad-Breasted White turkeys provided by British United Turkeys of America (BUT), based in West Virginia. The birds had daily access to outdoor ranges, forage, shelter and roosting facilities. Data was collected on weather, health, feed consumption, disease, mortality, weekly weight gain, dead weight and dressed weight, behavioural observation and sales.

The farm participants reported faster weight gain and improved feed conversion in the industrial line when compared with the Bourbon Red, which was expected. The Broad-Breasted Whites achieved their market weight in an average of 131 days, compared to an average of 185 days for the Bourbon Reds. Correspondingly, the commercial birds consumed an average of 5 pounds of feed per pound of weight gained, while the Bourbon Reds consumed 6.8 pounds. Both flocks dressed out (prepared for the consumer) at about 75% of their live weight.

The industrial line, however, experienced greater mortalities from transport stress, heat and disease. Mortalities for the industrial line ranged from 13 to 93%, averaging 46%. The Bourbon Red mortality rate ranged from 15 to 31%, averaging 21%. (Loss from predation was not included in the mortality calculations as such a death is not related to the bird's immune response).

The more active standard turkeys needed slightly different management techniques to keep them in their pastures and closer to home. The Bourbon Red hens were well equipped to fly, often escaping from their pens and both Bourbon Red hens and stags (in America these are called toms), began roosting at an early age, while the industrial stags were not interested in roosting. The Bourbon Reds were active foragers, covering the pasture and readily eating offered treats of fruit and vegetables. The industrial birds were more sedentary. They suffered in the heat, panting and seeking relief in the cool soil in the shade of the barn. While the Bourbon Reds sought shade, they did not exhibit the same degree of discomfort and physical stress from the heat.

Additionally, Dr. Robert Gogal, Jr., a veterinarian and immunotoxicologist at Virginia Tech., conducted a series of tests to assess the immune function of some varieties of standard turkey and

an industrial line of turkey. The standard varieties had significantly higher survivability when directly exposed to the diseases haemorrhagic enteritis virus and E.coli.

These studies clearly indicate that the standard varieties of turkey, by virtue of their genetics, do have more vigorous immune systems which do make them the obvious choice for free range production. They demonstrate the value of the genetic resources that are embodied in standard varieties of turkey and justify turkey conservation.

At present, turkey conservation is undertaken through living gene banks which means that the birds have to live and reproduce in order to keep their genes alive. Although there is ongoing research into poultry gene banks this form of conservation is not widely used and tends to concentrate on chickens rather than turkeys. In the paper 'Animal Genetic Resources Conservation in the Netherlands and Europe: A Poultry Perspective' by H. Woelders, C. A. Zuidberg and S. J. Hiemstra, the authors from the Centre for Genetic Resources in The Netherlands say that increased global use of highly productive breeds of farm animals has been coupled to a loss of genetic diversity in most species.

Throughout European countries various organisations and individuals are trying to preserve the genetic diversity of livestock in situ. In the case of poultry this mainly relies on hobby keepers but gene banks are gradually being established. In both France and The Netherlands there are limited collections of the frozen semen of rare poultry breeds.

Recent work has focussed on finding a suitable replacement for glycerol. This is used in the process of taking and storing semen but happens to be a contraceptive in the hen. However, straw freezing has been used with success and this method has helped to extend the collection of poultry semen to eleven rare breeds in the Dutch gene bank.

The Rare Breeds Survival Trust (RBST) in the UK and its sister organisation in New Zealand are not at present collecting poultry semen for their gene banks, in part because semen collection and freezing is problematic in these species. The American Livestock Breeds Conservancy (ALBC) does not include poultry in its gene bank but is working closely with the National Animal

Germplasm Programme within the United States Department of Agriculture who are conducting research on poultry embryos to assess the viability of such stored material. The ALBC says that currently the most effective measure for the conservation of turkey genetic material is with live animals.

Countries are now becoming aware of the loss of genetic diversity and there is an international obligation to protect our Farm Animal Genetic Resources (FAnGR) including the turkey. As one of 150 signatories to the Convention on Biological Diversity (CBD) at Rio de Janeiro in 1992, the UK has an international obligation to look after its FAnGR. The United Nations Food and Agriculture Organisation (FAO) Global Strategy for the Management of Farm Animal Genetic Resources, which the UK is a party to, is the international mechanism through which action recommended by the CBD is taken.

In response to this the UK Government, through the Department for Environment, Food and Rural Affairs (DEFRA) has produced a UK National Action Plan on Farm Animal Genetic Resources and is setting up a National Standing Committee on Farm Animal Genetic Resources to advise government on the future conservation and use of genetic diversity.

I therefore think that with this recognition there will be more input in this field but at present, I agree with the ALBC when it says that thoughtful stewardship of these agricultural treasures by today's breeders will ensure their availability for generations to come.

Chapter Eleven | Reaping the Rewards

The marketing of turkeys destined for the table is of vital importance if you are going to realise the 'harvest' that you have been working towards. You will have put time, effort and money into raising the birds to be of prime quality so you will need to market them effectively to make all that work worthwhile.

All too often people decide to rear some turkeys for the Christmas market and think about what they should have and how they are going to look after them, only to forget about how the turkeys are going to be sold. This is not helped by the fact that in the spring when you are hatching or preparing to buy in poults Christmas does seem such a long way away. Good marketing is, however, paramount and you should be thinking about that before even considering going into turkeys. How and where you sell your birds could in fact have a real bearing on what type of turkeys you should be rearing.

Today's consumers are being encouraged to buy locally where possible. This saves on food miles, helps the environment and sustains the local economy. Traceability is also a plus factor and this could certainly help if the public know or can even see where the turkeys are kept and how they are looked after. These points can help the smaller producer so go for turkeys that can be reared free range and try to market them in a way that makes your turkeys different from others.

Turkeys suitable for free ranging will either be the 'improved' birds that have been hybridised and selectively bred to have double breast muscles which produce the rounded breast that

Your free range birds will have a ready market as more and more consumers question the origins of their food and want to buy local produce.

consumers are familiar with or a suitable variety of the standard turkey with a high breast-bone and single breast muscle.

Free range commercial turkey growers will have the improved birds and often belong to organisations that work with you on marketing. The National Farmers' Union supports members in marketing their turkeys by running a turkey hotline in the run up to Christmas. This hotline is for public use to enquire where they can buy a free range turkey in their area. The hotline has a press launch so usually gets media coverage, brings the free range turkey to the public's attention and does help with turkey sales.

Producers benefiting from the turkey hotline may belong to The Traditional Farm Fresh Turkey Association and it is also possible to rear and sell a traditional farm fresh turkey under a franchise. One of the most well-known in the UK is the KellyBronze turkey franchise. There would be certain criteria to be addressed but the company do provide a comprehensive training programme to provide you with the skills to grow and process a small flock of free range turkeys ready for sale at the farm gate at Christmas.

Franchising is the leasing of a business system by its owner, the franchisor, to a trader, the franchisee. The lease is governed by a contract under which the franchisor allows, for the contract period, the franchisee to use its trade name, trade mark and confidential business methods, working to a business blueprint that has an established successful track record. In return the franchisee, who is an independent trader, sells the franchisor's product, following strict laid down operational procedures that cover price, quality, the location, size and layout of the premises, animal welfare and environmental considerations. The franchisor provides advice and support on all aspects of running the business both before it starts trading and continually thereafter. Some of the requirements are a tidy farm, to be within a 15 minute drive of a town with at least 50,000 inhabitants, to be located near a main road and to have 5,000 sq ft of covered yard available from June until Christmas. This is not a 'get rich quick' scheme but one which, over the years, should grow into a profitable niche business.

If going it alone is your preferred option then you could go for a relatively new niche market with the slower growing standard turkeys and provide the type of turkey that has been enjoyed for hundreds of years. You would need to market them with information on their history and educate the consumer on the conformation of the bird with its high breast bone because its shape will be new to them. Part of the marketing will be that although they do not carry the weight of the improved commercial birds there is still plenty of meat on the breast which is very flavoursome and slightly gamey.

Selling direct at farmers markets gives you an opportunity to meet your customers.

Eventually your sales will increase through word of mouth but initially you would need to work hard at the marketing to make it successful. Just because you have some first rate turkeys roaming around on grass does not mean that local people will be automatically queuing up to buy them come Christmas. Remember that although this may be a new project for you, all those people out there will have been buying their Christmas dinner elsewhere for many years and could very well be quite happy with what they have bought and, if asked, may be likely to buy from the same place again. These people are your prospective customers and you need to convince them that they will be getting a different and unique product from you which they can value, enjoy and perhaps feel good about the fact that they bought it locally.

Don't expect to beat the supermarket on price because you won't be able to and there will be many people whose purse will dictate where they buy their turkey dinner. Your turkeys will need to be priced up according to the expenses generated throughout their life; their cost from day-old to the Christmas box. You will then have to add some profit to that for there is little point in going through all the work to end up simply breaking even. People will pay for good quality meat, so that is what your turkeys will have to provide along with any thing extra you may decide to offer to give you a unique selling advantage.

Selling direct to the customer will bring the best profit because you are bypassing someone else's take of the profit share. It will also allow you the marketing plus of talking to the customer so that when any questions are asked as to the rearing of the birds you can personally reassure them. You could even have an Open Day in the late summer so that people can see for themselves the good conditions that the turkeys live in and, for many people, this would prompt an order for Christmas. The local radio might be interested in coming along, especially if they can chat to the public about how they think the turkeys are being reared because there is so much bad press about poultry meat production and this would be refreshingly different.

Remember, pictures paint a thousand words and can often summarise your whole ethos instantly.

Put a neat sign up advertising the fact that free range turkeys will be available for Christmas, specifying that orders are being taken. However, do check that you don't need planning permission for the sign! If it is only on display for a restricted period this is not normally necessary. Put a few lines in the parish newsletter and an advert in the local agricultural merchants or even in the doctor's surgery or at the vets if it is allowed. They might say no but if the answer is yes it could get you another customer or two. Barter and bribe them; a free dinner might almost be worth an advert if it is in the right place!

Increasingly, people like their turkeys all ready for the oven and presenting it with a small bunch of sage and parsley will make it look most attractive. Get some seeds planted early and even if you decide not to have turkeys you will still have the herbs for kitchen use. Herbs will look very attractive and you could go one step further and design a recipe leaflet for the turkey. Your family's traditional roast turkey dinner recipe and how to cook it, along with a modern recipe to make some leftovers into a most welcome meal would be a nice touch. Give yourself a logo or at least a memorable name – Forest Farm Free Range Turkeys, Widdecombe Heritage Turkeys or 'Johnson's Turkeys: Born from the past to delight now.' However, do beware of Trading Standards and make sure that you are able to back up whatever you decide.

If your turkeys are organic then the positive message that conveys with regard to health, the environment, animal welfare and taste needs to be communicated. Consumers perceive that organic food tastes better than conventionally reared so it is necessary to ensure that they are not disappointed but if the turkeys are reared well and on grass they should end up being absolutely delicious anyway. Organic markets need to be identified though and if someone in your area is already selling organic turkeys at Christmas it could be that your market is already taken. A good idea would be to see if there are any organic box schemes in the area that supply organic produce but not turkeys. If the box scheme producers would

Turkey eggs do not need to be stamped. However it is good to use the words 'free range' or 'organic' if applicable.

allow you to put a leaflet and order form in each box advertising your organic Christmas turkeys, it would give you an idea of any possible demand. You are, after all, half way there if these people are already buying organic. Health food shops may well let you advertise or a local butcher might be interested in having some organic turkeys for his shop.

By all means get the family involved in thinking how you could make your turkey dinners more desirable and marketable than others. It would be a great project but one which needs to be worked on long before you have to put any of the ideas into practice.

Make sure you dress the turkey up for the box, include recipes and even seasonings to make it more memorable.

As a cautionary thought do not try to rear too many turkeys to begin with. It is better to be successful with those that you rear and have contented customers ordering again immediately after Christmas and talking about how wonderful your turkeys were. A list of satisfied customers is always far more desirable than a long line of unsold turkeys. Around twenty turkeys would be a very good starting point and you would certainly learn a lot in the first year.

When you have determined your outlets, buying a chest freezer in the sales would be money well spent! Then, if you do have any turkeys left you can freeze them and the family can enjoy them throughout the year. What you must aim for is to sell them all at the price you need to cover the expense with a little profit on top. Don't be tempted to drop the price drastically if it looks as though

you may have turkeys unsold. You are not a supermarket and will almost certainly not have other products that can subsidise the loss. If you cut your price people will remember and expect a cheap turkey through leaving it late to buy come next year.

Chapter Twelve | Bringing it to the Table

If you do take the decision to rear turkeys for meat then you must also decide precisely how you will slaughter and prepare the birds. It is certainly a subject for consideration in the very early stages and possibly a decision best made prior to any final decision to start up your venture as you will be required to plan ahead carefully with regard to your legal responsibilities; this whole field is covered by legislation which you must incorporate into your business plan!

Slaughtering is never going to be a pleasant experience but it can be humane. It is your responsibility to ensure that you are fully prepared to carry out the task or, alternatively, to arrange for someone who is competent to do it on your behalf. It is an offence to cause unnecessary suffering to any animal or bird and, by law, you must have the knowledge and skills necessary to stun and slaughter each bird humanely and efficiently. If you have any doubts about your ability you must not attempt the slaughter of even a single bird.

In order to slaughter birds intended for sale to the general public you will require a poultry slaughterman's licence for certain methods of slaughter. This does not apply to killing by either neck dislocation or decapitation on the farm where the birds have been reared. To obtain a registered licence you will need to apply to your local Animal Health Divisional Office for a Certificate of Competence which will be assessed by an authorised vet and can cost up to £70. You will then need to contact the Meat Hygiene Service to obtain a slaughterer's licence for which there is currently a £20 charge.

The age at which turkeys are ready for slaughter will depend on the variety.

Initially you should undertake some practical instruction in your chosen method of slaughter and this can be done on a short training course at an agricultural college or other training facility. You could also train by working under the supervision of a licensed or experienced slaughterman or veterinary surgeon. Once your slaughter training has been carried out and the necessary equipment organised you will be well prepared for the task. Do remember when deciding on a slaughtering date to leave time for the birds to hang for about ten days before evisceration.

If a turkey is not fully developed at the time of slaughter it will not be in the correct condition for the table. This is an important point. If your customers are to be persuaded to come back for more, your turkeys will need to have had plenty of time to grow and, after being slaughtered, should have been hung effectively as well. The age at which turkeys are fit for slaughter will depend on the variety, when they were hatched, their environment, your management and their feeding regime.

Standard turkeys will need longer to develop than hybrids and you should aim to get your poults from the end of April through to the beginning of June at the very latest if you plan to have them ready for the Christmas market. Most hybridised commercial turkey poults are usually collected at the beginning of July.

Feeding the birds finisher pellets in their final weeks of development will help to prepare them and you can check to see how they are progressing by separating the feathers and looking at the skin, particularly on the breast. If the skin is creamy white then the bird is putting down some fat and will probably be fit for slaughter but if the skin is still fairly dark it is not yet ready. Continue to feed the turkeys until the day before they are to be slaughtered; it is better if they remain without food for twelve to eighteen hours prior to despatch. They must, however, have access to water. Do not starve them for longer than a day because they will begin to eat whatever is around them and even in this short time it could result in the bird losing condition. The feed on the day prior to killing should consist of pellets only and not wheat, because wheat takes longer to digest and the bird may not be empty when it comes to the slaughtering process. The reason you do not want feed inside the body is because, during the hanging, the crop could begin to smell and flesh near the intestines discolour, which would have a detrimental effect on the end product.

When the day of slaughter arrives, catching the birds should be done as calmly and quietly as possible so they are not stressed and do not panic. It would be a shame to have come this far only to have the birds scratch or bruise themselves and mark the flesh unnecessarily. When catching, never lift a turkey by a single leg. Drive it into a corner or a shed and grasp the shoulder of the wing furthest away from you and, with the other hand, grip the legs. Then lift it by releasing the hand from the shoulder and running the arm down the side of the body while still keeping a firm grip on the legs.

A small numbers of turkeys can be slaughtered by:
- Electrical stunning followed by bleeding
- Concussion stunning followed by bleeding
- Neck dislocation
- Decapitation

Electrical stunning
This involves passing an electric current through the brain causing unconsciousness. Hand-held, low-voltage electrical stunners are generally used on the farm for smaller numbers of birds. The equipment operates from a step-down transformer with an isolated output of 110 volts. The handset is manually operated with interchangeable or adjustable electrodes to accommodate the heads of different sized birds. The level of current must be sufficient to cause an effective stun which, in turkeys, would be 400mA.

Neck-cutting
Birds must be bled within 15 seconds of stunning and legislation requires that at least one of the carotid arteries or the vessels from which they arise should be severed. A faster death can, however, be achieved by using a ventral neck-cut across both carotid arteries and both jugular veins.

By law turkeys must be allowed to bleed for a minimum of two minutes before plucking and evisceration can begin. Always check that the bird is dead before beginning this process. Hold the eye open and touch the surface with a shaft of a feather. If the third eyelid moves wait a little longer. If this happens the turkey needs a longer time to bleed out.

Concussion stunning
This is a severe blow to the skull which renders the bird immediately unconscious until neck-cutting causes death. Specific mechanical equipment should be used for this procedure which applies a percussive blow to the bird's head rendering it unconscious. If the manufacturer's instructions are followed it should produce an effective stun and the death of the bird. When

this equipment is used to kill turkeys for 'commercial' slaughter it must be followed by neck dislocation or bleeding. If it is not available then concussion is not recommended on welfare grounds as an effective blow to the skull by others means is by no means easy to ensure.

Neck dislocation

Although it is legal to carry out neck dislocation without stunning, turkeys should be stunned beforehand because of the size of the bird and the difficulty in achieving immediate insensibility by neck dislocation alone. There are a variety of techniques and equipment that can be used for this method. Dislocation involves stretching the neck to rupture the spinal cord and damage major blood vessels. Under no circumstances should you attempt to kill a turkey by crushing its neck with pliers. This does not have the same effect as neck stretching and is considered inhumane.

Killing cone

A killing cone consists of a restraining cone in which the bird is placed head down with a clamp below which serves to dislocates the neck. This can be used for a small number of turkeys although the Humane Slaughter Association does not consider this method ideal.

Pole

This method is easier if carried out by two people. To manually dislocate the neck, hold the turkey by the legs and wing tips with the head and neck on the ground. A heavy stick or pole should be placed across the neck behind the head and firm pressure applied to the bar on either side of the head. The person holding the turkey's legs should then immediately pull the bird's body upwards with sufficient force to dislocate the neck.

Once confirmed dead pluck immediately.

Decapitation

This involves the severing of the head from the neck and should be carried out after stunning. Although it is legal to do this without stunning the bird it is not recommended on welfare grounds as the brain remains active for up to thirty seconds.

Plucking

Once the turkey has been slaughtered and is confirmed dead, pluck it straight away. Dry plucking by hand is so much easier whilst the bird is still warm. If it is left to become cold the skin will hold the feathers well and truly tight and plucking will be a nightmare. Tie the bird by its feet and hang it up so that the person plucking can stand to work and use both hands. Remove the tail feathers, the wing feathers and then move to the breast. After these there are the legs, then the back and finally finish off any areas that are not totally clean and tidy. Hang the bird in a cool room with a covering on the floor to catch any dripping blood. The turkey is descended from a wild bird and is therefore treated as game and the hanging, as with pheasant and other game birds, improves the flavour and tenderises the meat.

The environmental health department of your local authority may need to inspect and approve the premises in which you intend to eviscerate the turkeys and any storage area you propose to use following evisceration. Preparing the turkeys for sale should take place in a clean environment with washing facilities so that equipment can be thoroughly cleaned in between eviscerating each bird. You will also require access to separate hand washing facilities because the whole process of evisceration should be carried out as hygienically as possible. You are preparing food for human consumption and this is the reason for local authority involvement in the process.

Butchering

Lay the turkey on a clean table and cut the skin around both hocks so that the inner sinews are exposed. Then pull each leg so that the sinews are removed. This is a tough job. You can buy a manual sinew remover which makes the task much easier but deciding if it is worthwhile will depend on whether or not you intend to have Christmas turkeys in future years. Once the legs are off, complete with sinews, cut off the beard and slit the neck skin. Then, at the base of the neck, cut through the neck. You may need a large butcher's knife for this as it must go through the bone unless you prefer to twist the neck and sever the vertebrae that way. Remove the neck and head.

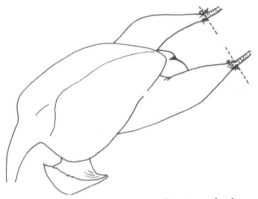

Remove the legs.

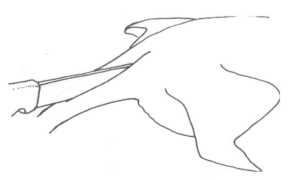

Slit the neck down to the wings.

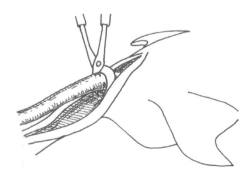

Remove the neck.

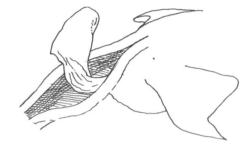

Remove the crop

Remove the oil glands just above the tail.

Cut around the vent.

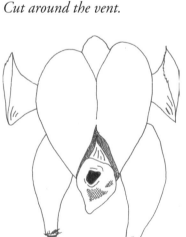

Pull out the innards and clean with a damp, clean cloth.

The insides are now clean with the heart and liver saved.

Holding the neck skin back, begin to ease out the crop and the trachea. Cut them off and discard. Then, remove the oil glands from the tail area and place the bird so that you can now cut horizontally above the vent area. From here your hand can work inside the bird to remove all the internal organs, intact if possible, because this prevents any accidental contamination. Make sure the carcass is clean and then gather the giblets together. Clean any debris from the heart and, along with the liver and neck (minus the head), place it in a bowl covered in greaseproof paper or foil and store it in a refrigerated area. These will be packed separately from the turkey carcass but supplied with it so that they can be used to make gravy. Some people also include the muscular part of the gizzard in the giblets but this is very much a personal preference.

All waste from the plucking and evisceration processes must be disposed of responsibly. The European Union Animal By-Products Regulation came into force on the 1st May 2003. It banned the routine on-farm burial and burning of animal carcasses and waste products and requires that any offal is disposed of through an approved route. This generally means via a renderer or knackerman, or using an on-farm incinerator. It is against the law to put waste generated from eviscerating turkeys into household dustbins destined for landfill.

Trussing

With about a metre of string, truss the bird by firstly looping it around the tail. Then bring the string from the tail around the hocks, pulling everything in as tightly as possible to tidy that end of the bird. Draw the string along the legs and, turning the bird over, secure the wings next and finally, tie these together over the back.

Cover the bird in greaseproof paper and place it in a refrigerated area that is to be used only for the dressed turkeys. Before the customer comes to collect the bird place it on some fresh greaseproof paper in the box in which you are selling it and place some herbs along each side of the breast and at the front. Cover the bird and insert your recipe leaflet in the box before securing the lid. Open up the box when the customer comes so that the purchase can be inspected. It is important that they see the product in your company and show approval before leaving.

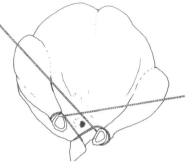

Truss the bird by firstly looping it around the tail.

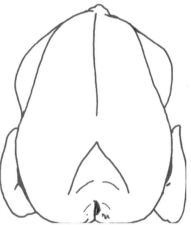

Turning the bird over tie the wings behind the back and it is then ready for your customer.

Not Just for Christmas..but..

You could make the collection day rather special by offering a mince pie and some punch around a Christmas tree with carols playing in the background. It may mean a few more pennies outlay but presentation is vital these days and as well as setting the right atmosphere for Christmas, if it helps to bring your customers back it will certainly be worth it.

Chapter Fourteen | Not just for Christmas!

Although the turkey is renowned for its meat people are increasingly recognising it as a very charismatic bird and more and more are now being kept as pets. By pets I mean a favourite animal that is considered a real companion although of course they do not actually live indoors like a dog or a cat. They would never be suitable for anyone living in a flat or with no garden; that would be inconsiderate as they do need space with grass in which to run around and explore and they will require turkey feed and housing, just like any other turkey. If a pet turkey has access to the house it will generally be quite clean but you have to be prepared for occasional little packages on the floor because, unlike a cat, they won't go looking for a litter tray.

In full feather turkeys are attractive, inquisitive, friendly and certainly intelligent if given the opportunity to be so. They welcome attention and are very communicative. It doesn't take long for them to pick up on what is going on around them; especially the fact that the person who feeds them often disappears into an interesting house very much larger than their own which can be accessed by simply walking through the back door!

Lonely is, very much a pet and is a prime example of a bird that has discovered where the hub of life goes on and it is in the farmhouse kitchen! Lonely isn't really lonely because he is too friendly a turkey to be so but he was called this because of being the only stag produced from a clutch of eggs. He has become quite a well-known character in Dentdale, Cumbria as there is a public footpath by the farm and walkers regularly meet up with him. It has come to the point where they even return with cameras so that they can record the handsome chap with a lovely personality who always has time to greet them.

Turkeys and other animals can co-exist but introduce with caution.

Elsie-May Phoenix watching day-time TV.

You might imagine that he is the sole bird and that is why he craves human attention but this is not the case. Lonely lives quite contentedly with a Pekinese, ducks, chickens and other turkeys. Visits to the kitchen are a daily occurrence and if it's a cold day he settles down in front of the Aga which dispels the notion held by some that turkeys are stupid!

Over the years I have received countless telephone calls about pet turkeys and it is very sad when some are unwell but the joy people get from the companionship of their birds is heart warming. Elsie-May Phoenix is one such bird which was constantly getting into trouble but since her demise she is greatly missed. Her owners say what a fun character she was. The Blue hen turkey would chase rabbits around the garden, would rush to the refrigerator if she saw you near it because her favourite treat was cheese and just loved being with the cats. "Yes, she was a turkey but we are glad to have known her," they told me.

I do know the feeling because I must admit to having a pet turkey myself. Petunia was rather disfigured when hatched, with a misshapen face and a twisted beak. Apart from this she seemed quite fit and full of life so was put into the brooder with the others. Poults, however, can be nasty bullies and were pushing her away from the feed, so she had to be removed. I put her into a box on the kitchen worktop with all the necessities where she could rest. Of course if I had been sensible I probably should have despatched her when hatched but by now she was looking like a game little character and it really didn't cost me much in time or money to let her live. Even with her concave face and crossed beak she could eat for England and she was determined that she was going to remain on the survivors list.

From her box I would take her and put her on my lap whilst I worked at the computer. As she grew larger she moved from my lap to the chair next to me and each day, after a long preen, she would settle down and nod off to sleep. Little turkeys like to perch on your wrist and this was quite an acceptable way of travelling from room to room, according to Petunia. When the pleasant spring weather came round again she would be taken outside to see and meet other turkeys as Petunia had to grow up realising that she was a turkey and not a human. By now she had a high opinion of herself and, being totally free around the smallholding, she would chatter and try to boss the other birds through the wire but every now and again she would come back to the house and sit in the porch waiting for me to open the door so that either I would go out or she could come in.

Petunia and the author.

When Petunia was a fully grown turkey I took her to be examined by Dr. David Williams, Associate Lecturer in Veterinary Ophthalmology at The Queen's Veterinary School Hospital at the University of Cambridge and it was agreed she should have an operation to enable her to open her eyelid more. After the usual nil by mouth, Petunia was taken in on a warm July morning for her operation. I wanted to try to improve her eyesight but to tell the truth I felt dreadful leaving her. The operation was performed successfully in the late morning and later that afternoon I went to collect her. She had been a dream patient but was still a little woozy and a quiet corner at home was what she needed. Eye ointment was administered for a few days to ensure that no infection set in and soon she was walking around the turkey pens no doubt letting everyone know that she was still in charge.

Petunia is a wonderful pet, a great character and a superb watchdog. If you hear Petunia's high pitched call it is because someone has arrived and she is not really sure if that is allowed. I had to put a saddle on her because love called and she occasionally made a bee-line for a Norfolk Black stag which also wandered around and I didn't want her to be harmed. The pleasing thing is that she knows she's a turkey and takes part in normal turkey life. When she started to lay eggs, of course, they were in some of the most inappropriate places; under hedges and behind the dustbins. However, after going broody I placed some fertile eggs under her for her to incubate and over the years she has successfully brought up several batches of poults. She is incredibly strict with them which is quite funny to watch, especially when they get to almost her size.

Petunia is very fond of living in Scotland but cannot understand why there are so many sheep around. Her latest venture is writing turkey stories for children so I am really pleased that I didn't do the sensible thing when she was hatched and gave her the opportunity to live and be creative in so many ways.

Chapter Fourteen | On with the Show

After having described the requirements for keeping turkeys, the trials and tribulations of their mating game, the preparation of birds for the table and even turkeys who think they are possibly human there is still one aspect of the turkey world which I want to share with you and that is exhibiting them.

Turkeys are definitely a part of the poultry show scene but this is in no way a new phenomenon. There is a long tradition of exhibiting turkeys which goes back well over a century. Classes for turkeys were offered at the first English Poultry Show in 1845 and the standard for turkeys appeared in the first English Book of Standards in 1865. The Slate turkeys were extremely popular as exhibition birds and in the early 1900s the Buff had acquired a tremendous following.

In the twenty first century Turkey Club UK establishes and maintains the turkey standards in Britain under the auspices of The Poultry Club of Great Britain. It is by these standards turkeys are judged at shows. They are integral to the conservation of the standard varieties of turkey and good examples of the different varieties are what turkey breeders work towards achieving.

Showing pure breed poultry is increasingly popular and can be enormous fun. There are certain rules and regulations that have to be adhered to but these are necessary to assist in the organisation of shows, to help them run smoothly, to provide the exhibitor with clear guidelines and for the welfare of the birds. Poultry shows are held across the UK and governed by the rules and

Prize Buff female from the 1930s
© Arthur Rice Collection.

conditions set out by The Poultry Club of Great Britain. There are small poultry shows, usually run by a regional poultry club or agricultural society with around three hundred birds on show; medium sized shows with up to a thousand birds exhibited and the very large championship national shows where almost seven thousand different birds will be vying for that elusive championship honour. At many of the shows there will be classes for turkeys but in the smaller ones it is usually one class for any variety of turkey male and another class for any variety of turkey female. At the large shows, however, each variety of turkey has its own class and there are even separate classes for males and females.

Turkey Club UK and the Poultry Club of Great Britain would be able to tell you where these shows are held and how to contact the secretaries. They are also advertised in specialist magazines. Decide on which show you would like to attend and request a show schedule in good time. When your schedule arrives look at your turkeys and decide which bird you will enter and fill in the appropriate classes. Then return the entry form with the details of your entry or entries, your name and address and the payment for each entry to the show secretary.

Most shows close their entries about a fortnight before the show but the large national show entries have to be in about six weeks beforehand to allow time to print the catalogue. It is certainly not a question of taking your turkey along on the day of the show and simply entering it there and then as all the penning for the birds has to be hired and erected and each entry has its own pen with a number on it. If you haven't forwarded your application on the entry form by the closing date, then you will not be allowed to exhibit. By the same token, if you have entered and do not take your turkeys there will be an empty exhibitor pen at the show.

There are tight biosecurity regulations for poultry shows and a licence from DEFRA is needed for them to take place. Contact details of exhibitors and their birds must be held by the secretary for a specific period and should there be any problem with an avian disease following the show the birds which attended are then easy to trace. No turkey less than one hundred per cent fit should be taken to a

Turkey 'Blue Boy.' Blue cock, 2nd Palace, 1st Cup at Birmingham in 1938 for Mr Keen of Devon.
© Arthur Rice Collection.

show. It should be clear of any parasites and should not show any signs of disease or injury. If the bird is not fit it would be unfair on both the bird and on the other birds at the show which it would be in close contact with. You would be asked to remove the bird from the show by the stewards if it was deemed to be unfit and you must also remember that it is actually illegal to transport a bird in that condition so in an extreme case you could face prosecution.

It is wise to decide well in advance how you are going to transport your turkey or turkeys to the show. There are various animal welfare concerns to consider and you may be required to have a completed Animal Transport Certificate with you in the vehicle depending on how far you are travelling to the show. Turkeys are not the easiest of birds to transport for the simple reason that they are so large. They should be contained in the vehicle both for their own safety and so that they cannot escape when a door is opened. A very large cardboard

Champion Turkey National Federation of Poultry Clubs Show 2004.

box with air holes cut into the top and sides for adequate ventilation would be suitable for a turkey or, in a large vehicle, you may be able to custom build a wire framed area complete with a top so that your turkey cannot jump out. Never transport a turkey in the boot of a car as there is insufficient ventilation and the bird could get extremely stressed. If you do so you could run the risk of prosecution if caught.

However you choose to transport the bird do make sure there is sufficient room so that the tail is not damaged. It would be such a pity to go to great trouble to prepare the turkey only to have a tail feather broken en route. Line the bottom of the box or other area with shavings so that the turkey is comfortable and does not slip whilst moving. Quite often, once you are on the move, turkeys will sit down because they soon discover that this is the best way of keeping their balance.

Preparation of the turkey is vital if it is to have a chance of winning a prize. You would normally carry out a regular delousing programme anyway but do this again about a fortnight before the show to make absolutely sure the bird is free of parasites. Turkeys do generally manage to keep themselves clean so a complete bath may not be necessary. If the bird does need a good wash do this a few days before the show so that there is time for a natural sheen to return to the feathers then keep the bird in a really clean area. Often only part of the turkey will need washing. This may be its rear but certainly its legs and feet and the beak could also need a wipe. You can stand the turkey in a baby bath or similar and wash it in tepid, soapy water, rinsing it

A Bronze prize winning stag from the 1930s.
© Arthur Rice Collection.

thoroughly afterwards. Use a mild baby shampoo, certainly nothing with detergent in it. The scales on the legs and feet can be thoroughly cleaned by using an old toothbrush to scrub them. This works very effectively.

Once you have washed any dirty areas dry them, first by towelling and then with the warm setting on the hair dryer taking great care not to use too much heat. If it happens to be an extremely hot day then the bird could be put out in a clean, contained area to dry naturally. However, it will take a long time for feathers to dry completely. What you must not do is to allow the turkey to chill through having wet feathers.

A turkey should take all of this in its stride if it is used to being handled. Do bear in mind that if it is not used to being handled it may not be suitable to be shown as the activity will unduly stress it.

The day before the show wipe a little baby oil over the turkeys face and neck. This will make the colouring come up really bright and shiny and help the bird to look really impressive. Wipe the legs and feet with some oil as well. If it is a stag with a beard, gently rub the tiniest dab of hair mousse down the beard between your fingers. This will highlight the colour and give it a fresh look without making it appear greasy.

Although some shows provide water containers in each pen for the birds, some of the smaller shows do not and you, as the owner of the bird, are responsible for its welfare at all times so do take some water containers along in case they are needed and don't forget some feed as well. A margarine container fixed to the wire pen with clothes pegs is quite adequate and large enough for turkeys if it is kept clean and topped up. Judging begins quite early on the morning of the show and it is normal not to feed the exhibits until after being judged but turkeys are usually given water and just a little feed to settle them. After judging they can have a good feed and some treats, so take something that you know your turkey loves, perhaps an apple or a cob of sweet corn.

On show day exhibits need to be in place by a certain time so give yourself plenty of time to get there. The worst scenario is being stuck in traffic and getting stressed about worrying that you will be late. On arrival, go and check the paperwork and see where your pen or pens are. The small shows usually have a photocopy of your entry form with penning numbers added to it waiting for collection at the secretary's desk. The large national shows will post your penning numbers to you well before the show so do remember to bring them and not, as I did on one occasion, leave them on the kitchen table!

Once you know where your turkey is to be placed, carry it very carefully but firmly, into the show hall. If it was boxed in transit it is better to get it out of the box and carry it because you will have more control over the bird and also because it's easier than carrying such a large box with a heavy bird inside. Place it in the pen and hopefully there will be sufficient time before judging for it to preen itself, fluff out its feathers and to make itself look really grand. Then wish it good luck and go and find yourself a cup of coffee; you will have deserved it.

A winning turkey on Championship Row with a mirror to keep him company.

A lovely part of showing is the social aspect and meeting up with people who share a similar interest to yourself. After judging, go and see how you have done. If you are given a placing it will make all the hard work and dedication to your birds seem so worthwhile and to get your very first card is a wonderful experience. To get your very first 1st prize will be fantastic and when you win Best Turkey you will be on cloud nine. There is always the possibility that the Best Turkey could end up being Show Champion but no one dare even think about that!

At the end of the show, take your birds home with precisely the same care as when you brought them. Ideally they should be isolated from the others birds for at least a fortnight to ensure that they have not caught any disease or other ailment. Give them another treatment of louse powder and, for a few days, put some feed supplement in the drinking water to counteract any stress they may have encountered. Even if everything goes to plan the change in environment will have been slightly stressful, as it probably would be for you. The turkeys may also be tired for a day or two so keep an eye on them but if looked after well they should be absolutely fine and will soon be communicating with their companions to let them know what clever birds they have been.

Then relax! If you have done well you will be looking forward to your next show. Even if you did not win a card you will still have learnt a lot and maybe next time you will do better. Experience will come with attending shows and learning from other exhibitors who no doubt will soon become not only good friends but friends who also understand the joy and hard work that are all part of a winning combination: you and your exhibition turkeys!

Appendices

Going by the Book

However you may choose to keep turkeys, whether as meat birds or as pets, they are recognised as a farm animal and therefore as livestock by the European Union (EU). The EU passes directives which then form the framework for laws across Europe. The UK Government then interprets and implements the European directives into British law and some legislation will have implications for turkeys. Below is a list of legislation which applies to animal welfare, how animals are dealt with when they are taken to market or to slaughter and transporting arrangements. There are also laws covering how food is prepared and how waste is disposed of. If you keep poultry and have fifty or more birds you must, by law, register with the Great Britain Poultry Register.

As legislation is continually being reviewed it is recommended that you obtain updated information from the following: the Department for Environment, Food and Rural Affairs (DEFRA), the Scottish Executive Environment and Rural Affairs Department (SEERAD), the National Assembly for Wales, the Department for Agriculture and Rural Development in Northern Ireland (DARD), the Trading Standards Department at your local authority or the regional Animal Health (formerly the State Veterinary Service) - which ever is appropriate.

Particular pieces of legislation which will probably require your attention dependant upon the scope of your proposed venture are the Protection of Animals Act 1911, the Protection of Animals (Scotland) Act 1912, the Welfare of Animals at Markets Order 1990 ("WAMO"), the Welfare of Animals at Markets (Amendment) Order 1993 and the Welfare of Animal (Slaughter or Killing) Regulations 1995 (as amended) (WASK) No 731. Under (2)1 of the regulation the term 'commercial,' when used in relation to slaughter or killing, means:

- In the course of or furtherance of a business or for reward.
- By, or on behalf of, the purchaser of an animal on premises belonging to, occupied by or under the control of the seller of the animal.
- In a market place.

WASK has itself been directly amended by several regulations. These are:

> The Welfare of Animals (Slaughter or Killing) (Amendment) Regulations 1999
> The Welfare of Animals (Slaughter or Killing) (Amendment) Regulations 2000
> The Welfare of Animals (Slaughter or Killing) (Amendment) Regulations 2001
> The Welfare of Animals (Slaughter or Killing) (Amendment) Regulations 2003
> The Welfare of Animals (Slaughter or Killing) (Amendment) Regulations 2006
> The Welfare of Animals (Slaughter or Killing) (Amendment) Regulations 2007

It is an absolute offence to cause or permit an animal avoidable excitement, pain or suffering. There are also specific rules on the handling, stunning, slaughter or killing of animals.

Both the Welfare of Livestock Regulation 1994 and the Welfare of Livestock (Amendment) Regulations 1998 have been replaced by a raft of new legislation which effectively implements EU Council Directive 98/58/EC, the so-called 'general directive.' Dependant on your location within the UK they are the Welfare of Farmed Animals (England) Regulations 2000 (SI 2000 No. 1870), the Welfare of Animals (Scotland) Regulations 2000 (SI 2000 No. 442), the Welfare of Animals (Northern Ireland) Regulations 2000 SI 2000 No. 270) and the Welfare of Animals (Wales) Regulations 2000 (SI 2000 No. 2682). These regulations cover all farmed animals and contain specific requirements such as inspections, record-keeping, freedom of movement, buildings and equipment and the feeding and watering of animals.

There are also regulations affecting food safety in connection with turkey meat. These are the Food Safety Act 1990, the Poultry Meat, Farmed Game Bird Meat and Rabbit Meat (Hygiene and Inspection) Regulations 1995 No. 540, the Food Safety (General Food Hygiene) Regulations 1995 and the Food Hygiene (England) Regulations 2006.

A further piece of legislation, the Animal By-Products Regulations 2005, prohibits the burial or open burning of farm animal carcasses or offal. Carcasses and waste should be disposed of through a knackerman, rendering plant, on-farm incinerator or pet crematorium. Pets may be buried but, as turkeys are categorised as farmed animals, a pet turkey cannot be buried although the decision here will ultimately rest with the local authority. For large commercial premises there is the National Fallen Stock Scheme whereby farmers pay an annual subscription and set fees per carcass for dead stock to be collected under the scheme and taken to a rendering plant.

There is also additional legislation providing the government with specific powers to bring in restrictions to prevent the spread of Avian influenza. This legislation includes the Avian Influenza (Preventive Measures) (England) Regulations 2006, the Avian Influenza (Preventive Measures) (Wales) Regulations 2006 and the Avian Influenza (Preventive Measures) (Scotland) Order 2007.

DEFRA, the Scottish Executive and the Welsh Assembly, backed by the poultry industry, have established the Great Britain Poultry Register in order to gather information about certain species of poultry held on premises in Great Britain. By law you must register if you own or are responsible for a poultry premises with fifty or more birds and this includes turkeys. The requirement applies even if your premises is only stocked with fifty or more birds for part of the year. At present, premises with fewer than fifty birds are not required to register but DEFRA is encouraging keepers to do so voluntarily. A registration form for the Great Britain Poultry Register or further information can be obtained by phoning 0800 634 1112.

The introduction of the Animal Welfare Act 2006 meant little significant change for turkey keepers as these birds were already covered by earlier legislation and the 2006 act referred specifically to pets. The Act does, however, have provisions for secondary legislation to be introduced regarding the welfare of farmed animals so there may be a number of changes in the future.

Welfare codes do not lay down statutory requirements. It is, however, a requirement by law to ensure that all those attending to their livestock are familiar with and have access to the relevant codes. Although the main aim of the welfare codes is to encourage livestock keepers to adopt high standards of husbandry, they may also be used to back up legislative requirements. Where a person is charged under the Agriculture (Miscellaneous Provisions) Act 1968 with causing unnecessary pain or unnecessary distress to farm livestock, failure to comply with the provisions of a welfare code may be relied on by the prosecution to establish guilt. A code of recommendations for the welfare of turkeys can be downloaded from the internet at: http://www.defra.gov.uk/animalh/welfare/farmed/othersps/turkeys/pb0077/turkcode.htm

The Welfare of Animals During Transport Regulation came into force on the 5th January 2007. This EU Regulation replaces the Welfare of Animals (Transport) Order 1997 which is now invalid. Under the Regulation everyone transporting animals must ensure the following:

- Journey times are kept to a minimum.
- The animals are fit to travel.
- Those handling animals are trained and competent.
- The vehicle and its loading and unloading facilities are designed, constructed and maintained to avoid injury and suffering.
- Water, feed and rest are given to the animals as needed and sufficient floor space and height is allowed.

For a leaflet on the Welfare of Animals During Transport Regulations, including details of the Animal Transport Certificate which may be required under certain circumstances, contact your regional Animal Health or the DEFRA website at: http://www.defra.gov.uk/animalh/welfare

All leaflets and further information on the above regulations can be found at the website: http://www.defra.gov.uk or via the address on the contacts page.

At present it is not a legal requirement to identify turkeys. However, if you wish to exhibit poultry on the Continent they are required to be identified by a closed ring and if you plan to breed with your turkeys it is immensely useful to be able to identify the birds. With tighter regulations regarding events where birds are brought together and traceability now being a greater requirement for biosecurity reasons, it is quite possible that in the future the Government may decide that pure breed poultry should be identified. This can be done by using either leg rings or wing tabs.

The Poultry Club of Great Britain runs a national ringing scheme and these rings are applied when the young poults are from about four weeks of age upwards. The art is to apply the rings when they will just slip on without coming off again but if they come off you can leave them for a day or two and then try again.

The rings should be placed over the right foot with the back toe held gently backwards against the legs and the three front toes held closely together. If the foot has grown a little too large, put some lubricant such as butter on to ease the ring over the foot. The numbers on the rings should be placed upside down on the leg so that they can be easily read from above. The numbers relate to the year of hatch and the identification of the bird. These are held on a database under the keeper's name and address. Turkeys need a J27 sized ring for males and a G22 size ring for females. Rings are registered on a computer to the first purchaser but can be transferred if ownership of the bird changes. At present the rings cost £2 for ten for Poultry Club members or £3 for ten for non-members, although prices should be confirmed on application. For a small fee six birds may be transferred from one owner to another. For further information contact the Poultry Club of Great Britain.

Alternatively, if you purchase adult turkeys with no ring then there are other identification means available. Aluminium metal rings can be fitted by a pair of pliers which lock the rings together around the leg. Various identification numbers can be printed on the ring or they may be ordered by colour only. Wing tabs are another means of identification and are very easy to fit by clipping through the skin. Metal rings, coil rings and wing tabs are available from poultry equipment retailers.

Useful reading:

The code of Recommendations for the Welfare of Livestock: Turkeys (PB 0077-1933) published by DEFRA is also available as a leaflet, free from DEFRA Publications tel: 08459 556000

The Code of Practice for the Welfare of Poultry at Slaughter (PB 3476-1988) published by DEFRA Publications.

Practical slaughter of poultry - A guide for the small producer, (2001, reprinted in 2004 with amendments) published by the Humane Slaughter Association. £2.00

A leaflet on The Food Regulations (2002), published by The Food Standards Agency, is available free from The Food Standards Agency Tel: 0845 6060667.

A Code of Practice for the On-Farm Slaughter and Marketing of Poultry (1997), published by the National Farmers' Union (NFU) and British Poultry Council (BPC) is available from both organisations.

The following Codes of Good Agriculture Practice are all available free from DEFRA Publications: The Water Code (PB 0585): The Soil Code (PB 0627) and The Air Code (PB 0618).

Glossary of Terms

Abdomen - underpart of the body from the keel to the vent

Ad lib feeding - poultry having access to feed at all times

Air sac - air storage areas that help to push air through the lungs

Airspace - small area in a newly laid egg

Albumen - the white of an egg

Back - from the base of the neck to the tail

Banding - different colour on an edge of a feather

Barring - horizontal band across a feather which is of a different colour to the feather itself

Beak - horny mandibles at the front of the face

Beard - a cluster of hairs not dissimilar to horse hair which protrude from the breast of a stag. In an adult stag it can grow up to 15cms (6ins) long. The hen does have a beard which occasionally is just visible but it is normally only a small stub of hair covered by the breast feathering

Biosecurity - Measures taken to prevent viruses, bacteria, protozoa, parasites, insects, rodents, wild birds or mites from infecting and affecting the health and wellbeing of your turkeys

Breast - the front of a turkey's body

Breeder pellets - a formulated feed containing extra calcium and vitamins for egg production

Breeding pen - 1. A male plus some females that are in the process of producing fertile eggs
        2. A housed and fenced area to segregate mating birds

Brooder - electrically heated area for very young poults

Broody - a hen which has the desire to sit on eggs to hatch them

Candling - looking at an incubated egg to determine if the egg is fertile. This is usually done after 7 days of incubation with a powerful hand held light

Caruncles - the fleshy prominences on a turkey's head and neck which can change colour from blue to red

Chalazae - two strands which help to keep the yolk of an egg the right way up

Closed ring - a ring placed on the leg of a young bird which cannot be removed later

Clutch - a number of eggs

Coccidiostat - a drug put in feed to prevent the growth of *Parasitic Coccidia*

Condition - the term applied to the state of the health and cleanliness of the bird

Crop - the sac-like organ in which food is accumulated before it passes to the gizzard

Crumb - immensely small portions of starter feed given to very young poults

Culling - reducing the numbers through slaughtering, either for health reasons or stocking density.

Caruncles and Snood.

Closed ring.

Defect - an imperfection but one which is not sufficiently serious to disqualify a bird from the showroom

Despatching or despatched - a term for killing poultry

Display - the act of showing off in a stag by fluffing up all his feathers, fanning out his tail and taking short steps in a jerky manner to impress hens. During this display he will also make a short guttural sound - 'puhhh' – which is air being released from the air sac. (Male snakes do the same.) Hens do not make this sound but do sometimes display and this can be just as impressive as the stag but a somewhat smaller version.

Dustbathing.

Disqualification - a serious fault or deformity that can bar an exhibit from competition

Down - the fluffy, hairlike covering of a newly-hatched poult

Double-breasted - a turkey which, by selected breeding techniques, has formed a double breast muscle

Dressed - a term for a carcass that has had the feathers and insides removed

Drinker - a piece of equipment that holds water for turkeys to drink from

Drums - a stag drums when he prepares for mating by fluffing his feathers, spreading his wings and 'drumming' on the ground with his feet

Dustbath - a container with dry soil or ashes for birds to use

Dustbathing - when a bird, usually a hen, rolls around in the soil flicking it over, usually to help remove parasites

Ears - holes on either side of the head

Embryo - the initial stage of becoming a poult following fertilisation of the yolk

Evisceration - the removal of the inside of a turkey (intestines etc.)

Faking - any unfair altering of a bird to cover up or remove a serious defect, evidence of which is an immediate reason for disqualification

Feather - one of the dermal outgrowths forming the plumage of a bird

Feed bin - storage bin for feed that is vermin and weather-proof

Feeder - a piece of equipment to hold feed

Femur - thigh bone

Fertile eggs - eggs laid by a hen who has been fertilised by a stag

Filoplumes - fine hair like feathers on the turkey

Finisher - a turkey feed given to turkeys that are intended to be slaughtered for the table

Flank - the side of the bird around the thigh area

Flights - (see also *Primaries*) feathers on the wing which are tucked up by the side of the bird when it is walking, standing or sitting

Fluff - the very soft feathers found on the underbody and around the vent

Fomites - inanimate objects that may carry and transmit infection i.e. clothing

Free range - a term used for turkeys that are able to wander around a very large area

Germinal disc - spot where the yolk is fertilised

Gizzard - the muscle where food and in particular fibre is ground up inside a turkey

Handling - taking control of a bird, also holding and feeling it to help determine its general condition

Hatching - the process of breaking out from the shell and becoming a poult

Head - skull, face, eyes, ears and beak

Hen - female turkey

Heterozygous - not true-breeding

Hind toe - back toe

Hock - where the femur joins the shank on the leg

Homozygous - of a genetic make-up to breed true

Horn colour - a rather pale creamy-gray translucent colour found on the beaks and feet of some birds

Markings.

Hybrid - commercial crossbreed

Hygienic - making sure that everything around turkeys is as clean as possible so that their good health is preserved

Incubation - keeping fertile eggs at a constant temperature and humidity so they can hatch

Incubator - electronically powered, thermostatically controlled, insulated box in which fertile eggs can be incubated

Infundibulum - funnel-shaped structure in a hen where the ovum is deposited and the chalazae added

Isthmus - part of the hen where the shell membrane is added

Keel - pendulous area below the breastbone

Keel bone - breastbone

Knob - the tip of the keel which is raised above the surrounding breast flesh

Litter - a covering used for bedding on the floor of the housing; usually wood shavings or straw. Sterilised wood shavings are available in bales from agricultural merchants and are preferable to shavings directly from saw mills as these may contain fungi if not sterilised. Fungi on wood shavings can result in severe respiratory problems

Longevity - the ability to live to an old age whilst continuing to be productive

Lungs - these do not expand in turkeys but have air pushed through them

Magnum - part of the hen where the white of an egg is added

Markings - the barring, lacing and other visible signs on feathers

Mating - putting a stag with hens for the purpose of reproduction and the act of copulation

Mixed grit - required to help the gizzard function properly and to give an added supply of calcium

Moult - annual replacement of feathers

Mossy - smudged markings making them indistinct

Mycotic - fungal (relating to fungi)

Nestbox - area where hens are encouraged to lay eggs

Organic - that which is natural

Oviduct - tube where the egg is constructed

Pair - a male and a female

Pathogens - harmful organisms

Pellet - various formulations of feed produced in very small baton shapes which turkeys can easily peck at and swallow

Pen - a fenced exercise area for turkeys, preferably grassed

Perch - a roosting place, mostly used overnight

Pipping - when the poult begins to break the shell before hatching occurs

Plucking - the removal of the feathers once a turkey has been slaughtered

Poaching - trampling of land when wet so soil becomes churned and muddy. Stagnant water can accumulate in the impressions

Poult - a young, immature turkey up to the age of 16 weeks when turkeys can be sexually distinguished with accuracy

Preen or coccygeal gland - small oil gland at the base of the tail

Perch

Preening - when a turkey is cleaning and tidying its feathers using its beak

Primaries - flights (flight feathers) which are tucked up at the side of the bird when not in use

Quill - the hollow stem of the feathers which attaches them to the body

Ration - a feed manufacturer's formulation for a species, and the different rations for different age groups

Roach back - a hump back which is a deformity

Saddle - item of leather or canvas placed on a hen turkey to protect her from being damaged by the stag during mating

Secondaries - the wing feathers which are still visible when the wings are closed

Self-colour - one uniform colour throughout the body

Set - to put eggs under a broody or in an incubator so that they can hatch

Sexing - determining whether a turkey is male or female

Shaft - the stem or inner part of a feather

Shank - the lower leg or metatarsus

Sheen - the metallic looking gloss on feathers, usually on a black or bronze plumage

Shoulder - the upper part of the wing nearest to the neck

Sinus - the area on the face between the eye and the nostril which can swell if infected

Sitting - a clutch of fertile eggs

Slipped wing - a permanently deformed wing where the primaries slip below the secondaries when the wing is closed. This will result in a standard disqualification

Snood - fleshy muscle on the face above the beak that extends when the stag displays and may be contracted to an inch long erect knob on the head when not displaying. Hens have snoods as well but these are only a small pimple above the beak and they do not extend.

Split wing - a wing where there is a noticeable gap between the primaries and the secondaries. This is a deformity and standard disqualification.

Sport - a new colour produced unexpectedly from a pure breeding pen of birds. A sport can be the result of a gene that goes back many generations.

Spur - the boney protrusion on the leg above the foot

Stag - a male turkey also called a Tom in America

Standards - a precise description of a breed or variety of bird which has been maintained over the years

Standard variety of turkey - one which has not been improved by man to form a double-breast, an original variety with a high breast-bone

Starter crumbs - a formulated crumb feed for day-old poults up until they are about 5 weeks old

Stocking rate - the number of turkeys in a particular area

Tail feathers - The stag usually has 18 main tail feathers.

Stockmanship - the skill of good animal husbandry

Strain - a particular group or family of birds that have been selectively bred by the keeper over a number of years

Stub - tiny, partly grown feather, that can be seen left on the flesh once a turkey has been plucked. Stubs need to be removed to be able to present a table bird that looks clean and neat.

Sunbathing - when a turkey, usually a hen, lies with outstretched wing and leg towards the sun

Symmetry - perfection of proportion in all parts of the body

Tail feathers - large, straight tail feathers which stand upright when the stag turkey is fanning them. The turkey usually has 18 main tail feathers but there can be one less or even two more.

Trachea - windpipe

Treading - when the stag mounts the hen to 'tread' her which induces her to co-operate and copulate

Uterus - part of the hen where the shell is added

Variety - a definite line of breeding which has distinctive colouring or markings and breeds true

Vent - anus

Wattle - the fleshy flap at the front of a turkey's neck which is surrounded by caruncles

Wing clipping - the process of cutting off the outer half to two thirds of the primary feathers, usually only on one wing, with secateurs or pliers to prevent flight. (With one wing clipped the bird is lop-sided and cannot take off). This can be done at around 8 weeks and again when fully adult and after regrowth.

Wing coverts - the feathers covering the roots of the secondaries

Wry tail - a tail always displayed at an angle, either to the right or left

Anatomy

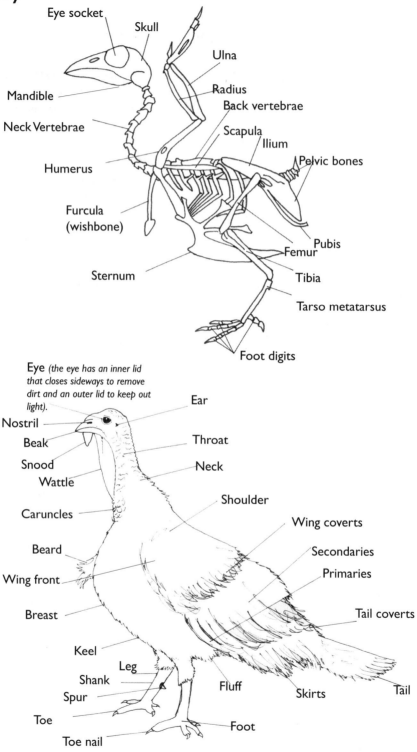

Eye socket

Skull

Ulna

Radius

Back vertebrae

Mandible

Scapula

Ilium

Neck Vertebrae

Pelvic bones

Humerus

Furcula
(wishbone)

Pubis

Femur

Sternum

Tibia

Tarso metatarsus

Foot digits

Eye *(the eye has an inner lid
that closes sideways to remove
dirt and an outer lid to keep out
light).*

Ear

Nostril

Throat

Beak

Neck

Snood

Wattle

Shoulder

Caruncles

Wing coverts

Beard

Secondaries

Primaries

Wing front

Breast

Tail coverts

Keel

Leg

Shank

Spur

Fluff

Skirts

Tail

Toe

Foot

Toe nail

And finally..did you know that..

• A hen turkey, depending on variety, can lay between 50 to 80 eggs a year.

• Turkey eggs are excellent for eating, either as themselves or in baking. The extra albumen makes really light sponge cakes and soufflés and the creamy yolks make great pastry sauces. They are not often seen on sale because it is more cost effective to turn the egg into a turkey for its meat.

• Benjamin Franklin wanted the national bird of America to be the turkey, not the Bald Eagle.

• A US Biological Survey counted approximately 4,600 feathers on a year-old black turkey hen, 5,600 on an adult black stag and an average of 5,523 on two small year-old white hens. In these counts the feathers were first picked and sacked and later counted. It is probable that during this procedure a number of feathers went uncounted. Therefore, a ten per cent addition to each of the above figures would probably bring the count closer to the actual number.

• In England turkeys used to be walked to market in flocks and wore tiny boots to protect their feet, or had tar put on the soles of the feet.

• Some highways are named after traditional turkey routes, such as Turkey Cock Lane.

• Native American Indians made turkey 'callers' and children were taught to be decoys in order to 'call' the wild turkeys towards the hunters.

• Turkeys have a wide field of vision - about 270 degrees.

• Gobbling turkeys can be heard a mile away on a quiet day.

• In the Guiness Book of World Records Vincent Pilkington holds the record for the fastest time to pluck a turkey. He took 1 minute and 30 seconds at Cootehill, County Cavan in Ireland on the 17th of November 1980. Vincent is so enthusiastic about his skills that he even carried out 24 hours of turkey plucking to raise funds for his Holy Family School, managing to pluck 244 turkeys in this time.

• A ballroom dance called the 'turkey trot' was popular in the early 1900s. It was named after the jerky steps that stag turkeys take and couples danced around in circles, bobbing their heads.

• Longbow arrow fletchings are made from standard turkey feathers.

• The Native American tribe to celebrate the first Thanksgiving with the colonists was the Wampanoag tribe.

• Israel is the country which consumes the most turkey per year per capita.

• Wild birds like to line their nests with the fluff of turkey feathers.

Useful contacts

Turkey Club UK
Janice Houghton-Wallace, Cults Farmhouse, Whithorn, Newton Stewart, DG8 8HA. Tel: 01988 600763, Website: www.turkeyclub.org.uk, E-mail: info@turkeyclub.org.uk. *Contacts for turkey saddles are available through Turkey Club UK*

The Poultry Club of Great Britain. **Mrs. Ann Bachmet, General Secretary/Treasurer, South Lodge, Creeton Road, Swinstead, Grantham, Lincolnshire, NG33 4PG, Tel 01476 550067, Website: www.poultryclub.org, E-mail: info@poultryclub.org.** *Umbrella organisation for breed clubs and responsible for organising The National Poultry Show where the club show for Turkey Club UK is held*

The Nat. Federation of Poultry Clubs. **Mr. A.D.Keep, Riverlea, 11 Oakley Road, Clapham, Bedfordshire, MK41 6AN, Tel: 01234 342656.** *Organises a championship show in December with a regional show for Turkey Club UK*

Scottish National Show. **Secretary, Mr. R.W.MacDonald, 4 Pine View, Mintlaw, Nr. Peterhead, Aberdeenshire, AB42 5GG. Tel: 01771 622557**

Kingsbridge Fur and Feather Society. **Secretary, Mrs. R.Brousson, Waterfoot, Tidal Road, Aveton Gifford, Kingsbridge, Devon, TQ7 4JN. Tel: 01548 550792.** *Organises a poultry show which includes a regional show for Turkey Club UK*

Organisations

The Anglian Turkey Association. **Secretary, Mr. Len Goodman, 19 Birkin Close, Tiptree, Colchester, Essex, CO5 0PB. Tel/Fax: 01621 815740, Website: www.anglianturkeyassoc.org.uk**

The Traditional Farm Fresh Turkey Association. **PO Box 3041, Eastbourne, East Sussex, BN21 9EN, Website: www.golden-promise.co.uk. E-mail:info@golden-promise.co.uk**

British Poultry Council (BPC). **Europoint House, 5 Lavington Street, London, SE1 0NZ, Tel: 0207 202 4760 Website: www.poultry.uk.com, E-mail: bpc@poultry.uk.com**

National Farmers' Union. **Agriculture House, Stoneleigh Park, Stoneleigh, Warwickshire, CV8 2TZ Tel: 024 7685 8500, Website: www.nfuonline.com,**

British Poultry Veterinary Association. **c/o British Veterinary Association, 7 Mansfield Street, London, W1G 9NQ. Tel: 020 7636 6541, Fax: 020 7637 4769**

Commercial turkey producers

Copas Traditional Turkeys Ltd. **Kings Coppice Farm, Grubwood Lane, Cookham, Maidenhead, Berks, SL6 9UB Tel: 01628 474678, Fax: 01628 474679. Website: www.copas.co.uk, E-mail: turkeys@copas.co.uk**

Kelly Turkeys & Farmgate Hatcheries. **Springate Farm, Bicknacre Road, Danbury, Essex, CM3 4EP Tel: 01245 223581, Fax: 01245 226124. Website: www.kellyturkeys.com,**

Government Departments and Agencies

Department for Environment, Food and Rural Affairs (DEFRA). Animal Welfare Division, 1a Page Street , London, SW1P 4PQ, Tel: 020 7904 6576. Website: www.defra.gov.uk. Farm Welfare desk Tel: 020 7904 6576, Slaughter desk 020 7904 6566, On farm poultry 0208 904 6515 and general DEFRA helpline 08459 335577.

Scottish Executive Environment and Rural Affairs Department (SEERAD). Pentland House, 47 Robb's Loan, Edinburgh, EH14 1TY. Tel: 0131 244 6482. Website: www.scotland.gov.uk

National Assembly for Wales. Cathays Park, Cardiff, CF10 3NQ. Tel: 0845 0103300
Website: www.wales.gov.uk

Department for Agriculture and Rural Development in Northern Ireland (DARD). Dundonald House, Upper Newtownlands Road, Upper Newtownlands Road, Belfast, BT4 3SB. Tel: 028 9052 4950
Website: www.dardni.gov.uk

Meat Hygiene Service (MHS). Headquarters, Foss House, Kingspool, 1-2 Peasholme Green, York, YO1 7PX
Tel: 01904 455 501. Website: www.foodstandards.gov.uk, E-mail: mhsenquire@foodstandard.gsi.gov.uk

Food Standards Agency. Aviation House, 125 Kingsway, London, WC2B 6NH. Tel: 0207 276 888
Website: www.food.gov.uk

Independent welfare organisations

Farm Animal Welfare Council. FAWC Secretariat, 5th Floor, 1a Page Street, London, SW1P 4PQ
Tel: 0207 904 6534, Fax: 0207 904 6993. Website: www.fawc.org.uk

RSPCA. Freedom Food Ltd, Wilberforce Way, Southwater, Horsham, West Sussex, RH13 9RS
Tel: 0870 754 0014, Fax: 0870 753 0015. Website: www.freedomfood.co.uk,
E-mail: freedomfood@rspca.org.uk

Training organisations

Lantra Connect. Lantra House, Stoneleigh Park, Nr Coventry, Warwickshire, CV8 2LG
Tel: 0845 707 8007. Website: www.lantra.co.uk, E-mail: connect@lantra.co.uk

AW Training. University of Bristol, Department of Clinical Veterinary Science, Churchill Building, Langford, Bristol, BS40 5DU Tel: 0117 928 9295. Website: www.awtraining.com, E-mail: enquiries@awtraining.com

Humane Slaughter Association. The Old School, Brewhouse Hill, Wheathampstead, Hertfordshire, AL4 8AN
Tel: 01582 831919, E-mail: info@hsa.org.uk

Meat Training Council. PO Box 141, Winterhill House, Snowdon Drive, Milton Keynes, MK6 1YY
Tel: 01908 231062. Website: www.meattraining.org.uk, E-mail: info@meattraining.org.uk

Poultec Training Ltd. South Green Park Enterprise Centre, Mattishall, Dereham, Norfolk, NR20 3JY. Tel: 01362 850983. Website: www.poultec.co.uk, E-mail: enquiries@poultec.co.uk.
The above cover all types of poultry training including management, welfare, slaughter and butchery.

Equipment

Accles & Shelvoke, Selco Way, Minworth Industrial Estate, Minworth, Sutton Coldfield, West Midlands, B76 1BA. Tel: 0121 313 4567. Website: www.acclesandshelvoke.co.uk, E-mail: info@acclesandshelvoke.co.uk

AI Equipment, 5c Cranmere Road, Okehampton, Devon, EX20 1QA. Tel: 01837 54944, Fax: 01837 54955

Brinsea Products Ltd., Station Road, Sandford, North Somerset, BS25 5RA. 0845 2260120, Fax 01934 820250. Website: www.brinsea.co.uk, E-mail: sales@brinsea.co.uk

Whitehead Engineering Ltd., 72 Haydon Industrial Estate, Radstock, Bath, Somerset, BA3 3RD Tel: 01761 432305, Fax: 01761 435329. Website: www.whiteheadengineering.co.uk

Current UK Organic Certification Bodies

Soil Association Certification Ltd, South Plaza, Marlborough Street, Bristol, BS1 3NX. Tel: 0117 314 5000 Fax: 0117 314 5001. Website: www.soilassociation.org, E-mail: info@soilassociation.org

Soil Association Scotland. 18 Liberton Brae, Tower Mains, Edinburgh, EH16 6AE Tel: 0131 666 2474 Fax: 0131 666 1684. E-mail: contact@sascotland.org

Organic Farmers and Growers Ltd., Elim Centre, Lancaster Road, Shrewsbury, Shropshire, SY1 3LE Tel: 0845 330 5122, Fax: 0845 330 5123. Website: www.organicfarmers.org.uk, E-mail: info@organicfarmers.org.uk

The Scottish Organic Producers Association, Scottish Organic Centre, 10th Avenue, Royal Highland Centre, Ingliston, Edinburgh, EH28 8NF. Tel: 0131 333 0940 Fax: 0131 333 2290 Website: www.sopa.org.uk, E-mail: info@sopa.org.uk

The Organic Food Federation, 31 Turbine Way, Eco Tech Business Park, Swaffham, Norfolk, PE37 7XD Tel: 01760 720444 Fax: 01760 720790, Website: www.orgfoodfed.com, E-mail: info@orgfoodfed.com

The Biodynamic Agricultural Association, Painswick Inn Project, Gloucester Street, Stroud, Gloucester, GL5 1QG. Tel/Fax: 01453 759501. Website: www.biodynamic.org.uk, E-mail: office@biodynamic.org.uk

The Irish Organic Farmers and Growers, Main Street, Newtownforbes, County Longford, Ireland Tel: (353) 043 42495 Fax: (353) 043 42496. Website: www.iofga.org, E-mail: iofga@eircom.net

Organic Trust Ltd., Vernon House, 2 Vernon Avenue, Clontarf, Dublin 3, Ireland. Tel/Fax: (353) 1 853 0271 Website: www.iol.ie/~organic/trust.html, Email: organic@iol.ie

Cmi Certification, Cmiplc, Long Hanborough, Oxford, OX29 8LH. Tel: 01993 885600 Fax: 01993 885 603 Website: www.cmi-plc.com, E-mail: enquiries@cmi-plc.com

Quality Welsh Food Certification. Tel: 01970 636688 Email: qwfc@wfsagri.co.uk

Ascisco Limited *This is a subsidiary company of the Soil Association set up in 2003 to offer organic certification to the minimum UK organic standards under the UK-15 programme. UK15 is available for all companies that require organic certification but cannot meet the full Soil Association standards. The Soil Association symbol may not be used on UK15 products.* Tel: 0117 914 2412. E-mail: prod.cert@soilassociation.org

Periodicals

Fancy Fowl, TP Publications, The Publishing House, Station Road, Framlingham, Suffolk, IP13 9EE
Tel: 01728 622030, Fax: 01728 622031.
Website: www.fancyfowl.com, E-mail: fancyfowl@todaymagazines.co.uk

Poultry World, Quadrant House, Sutton, Surrey, SM2 5AS. Tel: 0208 652 4911, Fax: 0208 652 4042
E-mail: poultry.world@rbi.co.uk

Smallholder, 3 Falmouth Business Park, Bickland Water Road, Falmouth, Cornwall, TR11 4SZ
Tel: 01326 213303, Fax: 01326 212084.
Website: www.smallholder.co.uk, E-mail: smallholder@packetseries.co.uk

Country Smallholding, Archant Devon, Fair Oak Close, Exeter Airport Business Park, Clyst Honiton, Nr. Exeter, EX5 2UL. Tel: 01392 888481, Fax: 01392 888499. Website: www.countrysmallholding.com

Bibliography

Biester, H.E.& Schwarte, L.H. Diseases of Poultry (Fifth edition, 1965, Iowa State University Press)
Bland, David C. Turkeys - A Guide to Management (2000, Crowood Press)
Collins, J.W. Turkeys (1954, Cassell & Co Ltd)
Christman C.J. & Hawes, R.O. Birds of a Feather – Saving Rare Turkeys from Extinction (1999, American Livestock Breeds Conservancy)
Eiche, Sabine Presenting the Turkey – The Fabulous Story of a Flamboyant and Flavourful Bird (2004, Centro Di, Florence)
Feltwell, Ray Turkey Farming (1952, Faber)
Klein, G.T. Starting Right With Turkeys (Edited by E.Robinson, 1947 Macmillan)
McMullin, Paul A Pocket Guide to Poultry Health and Disease (2004, 5M Enterprises Ltd)
Marsden, S.J. & Martin, J.H. Turkey Management (Sixth edition, 1955, Interstate)
Mercia, Leonard S. Raising Your Own Turkeys (1981, Storey Communications, Inc, Vermont)
Randall, C.J. A Colour Atlas of Diseases of the Domestic Fowl & Turkey (1985, Wolfe Medical Publications Ltd)
Roberts, Michael Turkeys at Home (1989, The Gold Cockerel Series)
Roberts, Victoria BVSc, MRCVS Diseases of Free-range Poultry (2000, Whittet Books)
Roberts, Victoria BVSc, MRCVS Ducks, Geese and Turkeys for anyone (2002 Whittet Books)
Sturkie, P.D. Avian physiology (Second edition, 1965, Ballière, Tindall & Cassell)

Some of the above books are out of print but may be found in a library or second hand bookshop.

Index

Farming Books and Videos Ltd.

Farming Books and Videos Ltd., is a family run, independant publishing company specialising in titles for the farmer, smallholder and country-dweller.

Other titles include:

A Cut Above the Rest DVD *covering the butchering of lamb, pork and poultry*
Basic Butchering of Beef DVD
The Sausage Book by Paul Peacock.
Traditional Cattle Breeds by Peter King
The Shepherd's Pup DVD
Talking Sheepdogs by Derek Scrimgeour
A Guide to Traditional Pig Keeping by Carol Harris
The Smoking and Curing Book by Paul Peacock
Jack Hargreaves - A Portrait by Paul Peacock
The Cheesemaking Book by Paul Peacock
Nature's Harvest by Paul Peacock
The Secret Life of Cows by Rosamund Young
The Polytunnel Companion by Jayne Neville

A full catalogue is available on request or visit our website for our full mail-order catalogue online.

Farming Books and Videos Ltd.,
PO Box 536, Preston, PR2 9ZY.
Telephone 01772 652693
www.farmingbooksandvideos.com